THE
GENERAL MANAGERS

THE
GENERAL MANAGERS
John P. Kotter

THE FREE PRESS
A Division of Macmillan, Inc.
NEW YORK

Collier Macmillan Publishers
LONDON

The Free Press
A Division of Macmillan, Inc.
866 Third Avenue, New York, N.Y. 10022

Collier Macmillan Canada, Inc.

First Free Press Paperback Edition 1986

Printed in the United States of America

printing number

1 2 3 4 5 6 7 8 9 10

Library of Congress Cataloging-in-Publication Data

Kotter, John P.
    The general managers.

    Bibliography: p.
    Includes index.
    1. Executives—United States—Case studies.
    2. Executive ability—Case studies. I. Title.
    [HD38.25.U6K68 1986]   658.4′09   86-441
    ISBN 0-02-918230-1 (pbk.)

Contents _____

Preface to the Paperback Edition _____

THIS BOOK IS THE FIRST of what has become a series of works on leadership in complex organizations. My second effort is *Power & Influence: Beyond Formal Authority* (Free Press, 1985). The third is in process as I write this.

It has been four years since I completed *The General Managers*. Reflecting on its findings, three things in particular stand out in my mind:

1. *The incredible complexity of executive roles, in terms of both information/decision making and people/implementation.* Contrary to so much written about management that implicitly assumes a degree of certainty and independence, managers constantly confront information uncertainty and must rely on others to help them accomplish almost everything they do.

2. *The degree to which general managers are specialists, not generalists.* The key way that successful general managers cope with uncertainty and dependency is through specialization. They focus their efforts on a company or an industry (or both) to reduce uncertainty and gain countervailing power over the dependent relationships within their chosen area.

3. *The importance of the overall pattern of career development.* Successful general managers develop, over a long period of

time and through many different experiences, the information relationships and skills needed to perform well.
General managers are neither ''born'' nor ''made''
through any single event; it's far more complex than that.

These conclusions have powerful implications for people just
starting a managerial career. For that reason, I'm delighted to
see this book published in paperback edition that is more
economically accessible to college and graduate students. It won't
provide them with simple answers. But I hope it will help dispel
some of the myths about executive jobs and success in business.

December 1985   J.P.K.

Preface _____

OVER THE PAST SIX YEARS, a number of people have generously helped me with the project on which this book is based. Foremost among them are the managers who participated in the study, the administration within the Division of Research at Harvard Business School (Richard Rosenbloom, Ray Corey, Joanne Segal), and the leadership in the Organizational Behavior area here at HBS (Jay Lorsch and Paul Lawrence).

Others who have read and commented helpfully on drafts of this manuscript include Joe Bower, Richard Boyatzis, Al Chandler, Jim Clawson, Alan Frohman, Jack Gabarro, Richard Hamermesh, Paul Lawrence, Jay Lorsch, Morgan McCall, Mike McCaskey, Bob Miles, Andrew Pettigrew, Vijay Sathe, Len Schlesinger, Carol Schreiber, Jeff Sonnenfeld, John Stengrevics, and Rosemary Stewart. Their ideas have significantly enriched this book.

J. P. K.

1

Introduction

FOR MOST OF HUMAN HISTORY, people have depended upon themselves, farmers, craftsmen, traders, and landlords for the goods,
services, and employment they needed. This is no longer true.
Today people in the developed countries depend primarily on
managers.

Virtually all the goods and services we need for our existence
and for our enjoyment are produced by organizations that are
controlled by managers. This was far from the case as recently as
150 years ago. Today, almost all "working" adults spend half of
their nonsleeping lives being directed by managers. One hundred
and fifty years ago, less than 10 percent did so. A century ago,
many if not most people could reasonably say that the world's
business managers did not really affect their lives in significant
ways. Almost no one can say that today. In his discussion of modern management in the Pulitzer Prize-winning book, *The Visible
Hand,* Alfred Chandler writes that "rarely in the history of the
world has an institution grown to be so important in so short a
period of time."[1]

Yet despite the importance of modern managers to our present and future, because they are such a recent development, we
know relatively little about them—about who they are, what they
do, and why some are more effective than others.[2] And what we

do know, or think we know, very rarely comes from the systematic study of real managers in any depth.[3] This is particularly true for higher-level business managers—those charged with most of the responsibility for running an enterprise. Incredibly, there have been only two really in-depth studies of a group of top-level business executives, one by Sune Carlson in the late 1940s[4] and one by Henry Mintzberg in the 1960s.[5] And Mintzberg recently noted that his pioneering book, *The Nature of Managerial Work*, "exposes perhaps one percent of the proverbial iceberg."[6]

This book attempts to chip away at another piece of that iceberg. It seeks to do so by reporting and discussing the implications of a study of a group of *executives in generalist or general-management jobs: that is, individuals who hold positions with some multifunctional responsibility for a business (or businesses).*[7] Conducted between 1976 and 1981, this investigation employed multiple methods to look in depth at fifteen general managers from nine different corporations spread out across the United States. Although modest in scope by many standards, this is nevertheless the largest study of its kind ever conducted.[8] (A description of the specific objectives and the research process itself can be found in Appendix A.)

The Participants in the Study

The people selected to participate in this inquiry were general managers in a number of different corporate and business settings (see Figure 1.1). Brief résumés on all of them can be found in Appendix D, which has been designed to help the reader keep track of individuals as their names reappear throughout the book.

Because of the significant amount of time and effort involved in studying each person—typically, almost a month of my time spread over the course of a year—the inquiry was limited to fifteen individuals.[9] The specific participants (and companies) chosen were selected with three criteria in mind: (1) each had to have a GM job; (2) there had to be some evidence that they were performing well in those jobs; and (3) the overall group had roughly to mirror the very diverse pool of corporate settings from which it was drawn.

The participants ranged in age from thirty-six to sixty-two. The average age was forty-seven. Seven had bachelors' degrees (only), the rest had masters' degrees. All were U.S. citizens, al-

THE 15 GENERAL MANAGERS

—All with some profit-center responsibility

—All with some multifunction responsibility

—From nine different corporations

—Located across the United States

—Average 1978 compensation (salary & bonus) = $150,000

—Average age = 47

THE BUSINESS FOR WHICH THE GMS WERE RESPONSIBLE

Industries	Number of Participants	Yearly Revenues (1979)	Number of Participants
Manufacturing		$1 billion or greater	2
Consumer Products	1	$100 million–$1 billion	3
High Technology	2	$50 million–$100 million	3
Other	3	$10 million–$50 million	4
Nonmanufacturing		$1 million–$10 million	3
Banking	2		15
Communications	3		
Professional Services	2		
Retailing	2		
	15		

THE CORPORATIONS FOR WHICH THEY WORKED

Business Mix	Number of Companies	Size (1979 Revenue)	Number of Companies
Single business	2	$5 billion or more	2
Dominant Business	4	$1–5 billion	3
Diversified			
(Related business)	2	$100 million–$1 billion	2
Diversified			
(Unrelated business)	1	$100 million or less	2
	9		9

FIGURE 1.1.   A profile of the participants, the businesses for which they were responsible, and the corporations for which they worked

though one was born in Europe. Most major religions found in the United States were represented in the group, but there were no women or blacks. (As of this writing, less than 1 percent of all general managers in the United States are women or blacks.) The GMs were spread across the United States: five were in New England, two in New York, four in the Midwest, one in the South, and three in California. All were married or engaged, and all had children.

Although all fifteen GMs had jobs with considerable responsibility—the average 1978 compensation (salary and bonus) was about $150,000 per year—there was a wide range in the scope of their domains. A few people had over 10,000 employees reporting, through others, to them. Some had only a few hundred. A few dealt with budgets of over $1 billion, while one controlled a budget of only a few million dollars. The most typical job title was "Division President," but even here there was considerable diversity. Only one of the GMs was actually the overall head of his company; most were "divisional general managers."

The companies for which these men worked ranged from young (started in the 1950s) to old (250 years), and from big (yearly revenues of $10 billion) to small (yearly revenues of $10 million). All of the companies were moderately successful; none was on the verge of collapse. But some were much more profitable and growing much faster than others.

The industries these companies were in included: auditing and consulting; commercial finance; consumer small appliances; copiers; department-store retailing; investment management; magazine publishing; newspaper publishing; printers and plotters; pumps; retail banking; rubber and chemicals; specialty retailing; television; and tire and rubber. Many of the major aspects of the American economy were in some way represented.

Because of this range of people and GM jobs, it is hard to talk about the "typical" participant. Nevertheless, a brief description of a few of them can give one a flavor for what these participants are like. (A detailed description of these people and their jobs will be found in Chapters 2 and 3; brief résumés are in Appendix D.)

A Few Examples: Gaines, Thompson, and Richardson

Chuck Gaines[10] was the president of one of three major divisions of a very large midwestern manufacturer. He was responsible for revenues in the billions of dollars and had a salary above $150,000 per year. Although he did not have all his business functions reporting to him, he was responsible for coordinating all of them. His title was "Executive Vice President and Division Manager."

Chuck was born in a large, eastern U.S. city, the youngest of three children. He was raised outside the United States, but attended high school and college in the East. He began working for his current employer immediately after service in the Coast Guard and was married shortly after that. His career had taken him to three countries outside the United States, in addition to a number of locations inside this country. In 1979, he lived with his wife and eighteen-year-old son (a daughter was in college) a short distance from his corporate headquarters.

At age fifty, Chuck was a large and athletic-looking man. He gave the impression of being determined, forceful, ambitious, hard working, and cool under fire. More than most executives I've known, he clearly seemed both very powerful and very willing to use that power.

John Thompson was the head of the commercial finance division within a large eastern bank. His title was "Senior Vice President," and he was responsible for about 500 employees. John was located at the bank's headquarters and relied on corporate staff services in addition to his own people. His 1979 income was a little under $100,000.

John was born into a Methodist family in 1930 and raised along with his older brother in a small eastern city. After college and the army, he worked for ten years with one large manufacturing firm, then switched to his current employer. In 1979, he lived with his wife of seventeen years and two children (ages fifteen and twelve) in a rural suburb about twenty-five miles from work.

John was a bright, energetic, and well-organized executive who had an unfailing good sense of humor. He did not appear to be aggressively ambitious or forceful as Gaines. But like the others, he obviously enjoyed his job and was well thought of by his employer.

Michael Richardson was the president and chief executive officer (CEO) of an investment management company. This corporation employed about 200 people, many of whom had graduate degrees. Michael's 1979 income was over $150,000.

Richardson was born in 1934, the fourth of six children in a

Catholic family. He was educated at Ivy League schools and started work in the investment management field immediately after receiving his MBA. In 1961, he and four other people founded his current company. After working as a portfolio manager and a vice president of marketing for fifteen years, Richardson became president and CEO of that firm. In 1979, he lived with his wife and two children in an urban location a short distance from his office.

I found Michael to be an intelligent, sensitive, and sophisticated individual. Like Gaines, he worked long hours and was very ambitious. Like Thompson, he had a broad sense of humor and was extremely well organized.

The Findings and Their Presentations: Some Initial Comments

The Organization of the Book

The patterns found in the comparative analysis of the data on these general managers are presented in the following chapters. Roughly, these chapters answer the following questions in this order:

- Chapter 2: What are general management jobs really like? How much and why do they vary in different situations?
- Chapter 3: What kinds of people become general managers? How are they similar and different, and why?
- Chapter 4: In what ways do the GMs behave similarly? What common patterns exist in how they approach their work and what they do each day?
- Chapter 5: In what ways do the GMs behave differently? What causes these variations?
- Chapter 6: In light of the main findings in the study, what are the key implications for corporate selection, development, and staffing practices? For managing general managers? For the role of formal management education? For management theory and research?

Because some of the GMs in the study were performing better than others (see Appendix E for a detailed description of how performance was measured), throughout the book we will also address questions such as: Why do some of the GMs perform better than others? How much do differences in performance relate to differences inherent in the jobs and their business contexts? How much do performance differences relate to the different personal characteristics of the GMs? How much do performance differences relate to behavior?

Also throughout this book you will find about a half-dozen recurrent themes. These themes relate to size and scope, variety and diversity, specialization and fit, history and development, a necessary lack of "professionalism," and understandable complexity. In many ways, these themes represent the key findings from this study.

The Major Themes

One is struck when looking at the information gathered in this study by the sheer magnitude of many things. The demands associated with the GM jobs (discussed in Chapter 2) were usually severe by most standards. Even the "smallest" of the GM jobs presented the incumbent with significant intellectual and interpersonal challenges and dilemmas. Likewise, the number of personal assets (discussed in Chapter 3) that the GMs brought to their work to help them cope with those demands was very large. There is no evidence that it was only (or mainly) due to drive, or interpersonal skill, or business knowledge that these GMs were successful. Instead, a large number of motivational, interpersonal, temperamental, cognitive, and other factors seem to have been important. In a similar vein, there is no evidence that any single thing that they did was of central importance by itself. Rather, they all did a lot of things in their approaches to their jobs and in their daily behavior (discussed in Chapter 4) that helped them mobilize their considerable assets to cope with significant job demands.

One is also struck in looking at the information from the study by the great variety and diversity. Despite the fact that all fifteen individuals were in GM jobs in U.S. business corporations, the differences among these people and their situations were in many ways greater than the similarities. The key demands associated with their jobs, the personal characteristics of the GMs, the way they approached the work, and what they did each day, were sometimes radically different. As such, two GM situations that look very similar on the surface in reality can be very different. And two very successful general managers can be very different in terms of their personal characteristics and behaviors. We will examine in some detail an example of two very different GMs in Chapter 5.

A third theme that emerges in the data and is found throughout this study relates to specialization and "fit." The GMs tended to think of themselves as "generalists." Many felt they had the skills to manage nearly anything well. Yet in reality, they were all highly specialized in many ways. They had specialized sets of interests, skills, knowledge, and relationships. These specialized personal assets allowed them to behave in ways that fit the demands of their specific situations. It appears that this specialization and fit was central in helping them to perform well despite very difficult job demands.

A fourth theme that runs through this book relates to history and development over time. To understand the large and diverse demands associated with these jobs, the personal characteristics of the GMs, and their behavior, one needs to take a long view of things. The nature of the demands associated with these jobs is a direct function of some basic trends that go back fifty to one hundred years. The many personal characteristics that helped contribute to good performance in these GM jobs were developed over the entire period of these people's lives: during their childhood years, through their formal education, and in their early careers. As such, the basic behavioral style of the typical GM had deep roots and did not change much over time.

A fifth theme relates to how poorly the popular conception of the "professional manager" fits these successful executives. For example, if "professional management" means, as one writer recently suggested,[11] the ability to manage nearly anything well by relying on universal principles and skills and not on detailed knowledge of the specific business involved and close relationships with specific people involved in that business, then *not one* of the effective executives in this study was a "professional manager." Furthermore, if a professional approach to a GM job is characterized by the development of formal strategies and structures in a well-organized, proactive, and reflective way, then none of these managers behaved very professionally. Nevertheless, this "not professional" behavior worked, and it worked for reasons that are easy to see if one has a realistic understanding of the complex nature of GM jobs today.

A sixth and final theme relates to what one might term "understandable complexity." Complexity is without question the overwhelming issue here. The data show a complexity which often makes many managerial textbook concepts seem woefully inadequate. They also show a level of complexity which even the general managers themselves had difficulty consciously understanding. Indeed, as we shall see, these very successful general managers often had great difficulty explaining what it was they did, why, and why that worked as well as it did.[12] Yet despite this complexity, there are many identifiable and interesting patterns here. That is, despite the fact that management at this level looks far more like an art than a science, there are many identifiable regularities. It *is* possible to generalize. One can systematically study this important phenomenon.

To begin to make sense of these jobs, of these people, of what they do, and why it works or does not work, we need to proceed somewhat slowly and systematically. Step number one will be to look at the jobs themselves.[13]

2

The General Management Jobs: Key Challenges and Dilemmas

IT IS WELL RECOGNIZED in a general sense that the world of the typical manager has changed considerably during this century as organizations have grown larger, more diverse, more geographically dispersed, more technologically sophisticated, and the like. But I wonder if we really appreciate in a more specific sense how these trends, which continue today, affect the nature of managerial work.

With respect to general-management jobs, these trends seem to have made most of these jobs extremely demanding, difficult, and complex in both an intellectual and an interpersonal sense. These jobs today put a person in a position where he is held responsible for a complex system which he cannot directly control and cannot entirely understand. They demand that he identify problems and solutions in an environment where behavior-results linkages are unclear, that he cope with the fact that thousands of diverse issues and problems could absorb his time and attention, that he balance the short and the long run despite pressures to ignore the latter, that he somehow motivate good performance and deal with bad performance on the part of large numbers of subordinates, that he keep a very diverse group of people working together harmoniously and effectively, and that he get a lot of other busy people over whom he has no formal authority always to cooperate with him.

These same trends have also helped create more kinds of GM jobs, and have made the key demands associated with those jobs less and less similar in different contexts. As a result, two general-management jobs today can be very different in terms of the key tasks involved, and thus in terms of the demands they make of the general manager. Even GM jobs that look very much alike on the surface can present the incumbent managers with a very different set of challenges and dilemmas.

In this chapter we will examine in some detail the basic nature of the demands associated with all the general-management jobs in this study. Further, we will explore how and why these demands can be different in different settings.

The Job, the Context, and the Emergent Demands

Like most "jobs" in modern organizations, the GM jobs in this study tended to be defined, sometimes formally and sometimes not, in terms of a set of responsibilities and a set of relationships. Specifically, the responsibilities and relationships associated with these jobs were:

A. Responsibilities
   1. Long run—for setting some or all of the basic goals, directions, and priorities for an organization, including deciding what business or businesses to be in, and how to secure key resources.
   2. Medium run—for deciding how to allocate resources effectively to that business or those businesses so as to achieve long-run goals.
   3. Short run—for the efficient use of the human, financial, and material resources employed in that business or those businesses, including some profit responsibility.
B. Relationships
   1. Up—reporting to a GM boss (or a board of directors).
   2. Lateral—sometimes (but not always) having to rely on other internal groups for support (e.g., corporate staff) or having to coordinate groups that are associated with the business but do not report to this GM position.

3. Down—authority over what is usually a very diverse set of
subordinates (not just specialists in a single function).[1]

As the above suggests with such words as "some," "usually,"
and "sometimes," there was variety in how these jobs were defined, and we will explore that variation later in this chapter. But
despite that variety, this statement of responsibilities and relationships basically describes all the GM jobs in this study.

These jobs were located within broader business and organizational contexts that were almost always quite complex, owing to
factors such as business uncertainty and the large number of people involved. As a result, each of the job responsibilities and relationships tended to be magnified and shaped into important and
difficult sets of demands, challenges, and dilemmas.

*Job Demands I: Challenges and Dilemmas Associated
with the Responsibilities*

1. *Key Problem/Challenge #1: Setting basic goals, policies, and
strategies despite great uncertainties.* In the typical GM job in this
study, the long-run task was fraught with great uncertainty. The
number of factors relevant to this type of strategic decision making was generally enormous. Knowledge of how those factors
interacted was generally very limited. And tools for forecasting
those factors into the future were generally crude. Yet despite all
this uncertainty, the GM job was usually charged with overall
responsibility for making the long-run decisions for some organization.

Dan Donahue, for example, had been in the process of re-
examining and adjusting the basic direction of his organization
when I first met him. This reexamination occurred because his
division (which he had just recently joined) had been losing
money. The reexamination had proved to be a very difficult task
for two major reasons. First, Dan lacked clear information regarding the past and present state of affairs in his division and in
that industry. He could not clearly identify what, if any, distinctive
competence and comparative advantages his division had over
companies with whom they competed. Different individuals in
the company had varying opinions, none of which could be
objectively verified with available information. Second, forecasting future opportunities and risks was hampered by dozens of

important unknowns. Even the most sophisticated information gathering, analysis, and forecasting could offer only vague guesses to such questions as:

- Will there be any breakthroughs in the next decade in the two or three technologies they used most often? If yes, how will these affect product design and manufacturing economics?
- How will changes in the demographics of the labor force, in family patterns, and in disposable income affect consumer demand for their products? What impact will inflation have on consumer demand? How bad will the inflation be?
- Will any major new competitors enter their industry in the next decade? If yes, who are they likely to be (foreign or domestic) and where will they try to position themselves?
- Who is likely to win the U.S. elections in 1980 and 1984? What effect might that have on the regulation of their industry?
- What will probably be happening in the parent corporation over the next decade? How will that affect their inclination to provide resources to this division?

Although the long-run decisions that Donahue faced were extremely complex and the uncertainties very large, his situation was not at all atypical in this study. Indeed, at least half the other GMs had to deal with a long-run task which seemed to be as or more complex and uncertain. Furthermore, all the evidence of which I am aware suggests that the same is true in general for these kinds of jobs in corporations today.[2]

2. *Key Problem/Challenge #2: Achieving a delicate balance in the allocation of scarce resources among a diverse set of functional and business needs. Not allowing short-run concerns to dominate long-run ones, or marketing issues to stifle production needs, etc.* Because of growth, ambitious goals, performance problems, and the like, resources were usually scarce in the situations in this study. Indeed, none of the fifteen GMs had extra cash for which there was no clear need. This scarcity made resource allocation an especially important task. Furthermore, the typical situation had a diverse set of activities that required resources because of the different products, markets, functions, and technologies involved. This diversity made resource allocation a complex task. Taken together, scarcity of resources and diversity of needs made the resource allocation

task a most demanding balancing act. Under these conditions it was easy for short-run concerns to dominate long-run issues, or one product line to starve another, or one functional area to stifle another.

When I was with John Thompson, the United States economy had just gone into an economic downturn. Because sales were slipping, he had to reduce the resource budgets that had been previously planned in order to maintain some minimum level of profitability. In commenting on this, he told me:

> Sometimes it is very difficult to judge how much to cut and where in a situation like this. If I cut too much, we do well this year, but it will hurt us in the future. If I don't cut enough, we can be hurt badly this year. If I overdo the cuts in operations, we could end up with business that we cannot handle. If I overdo the cuts in sales, we could end up with excess capacity in operations. It really is a tough balancing act.

Frank Firono talked about this same basic issue in this way:

> In our business it is easy to crank out the short-term sales and relatively easy to get short-run profits. It's also relatively easy to get one store really performing well. What is difficult is to achieve acceptable short-run numbers while maintaining or increasing the quality of the business (a key long-term objective), and to get most or all of your stores performing pretty well.

To some degree, all the GMs in this study faced this problem. Evidence from elsewhere again suggests that this is probably the case for GM jobs in general.[3]

3. *Key Problem/Challenge #3: Keeping on top of a very large and diverse set of activities. Being able to identify problems ("fires") that are out of control and to solve them quickly.* Because the buck stops at the GMs' desks, any problem associated with their businesses can become their problem. Any task that is not being accomplished effectively or efficiently can eventually create serious problems for them. But because of the typical scope of a GM's job, spotting fires that are out of control can be extremely difficult. And because of the diversity and complexity of these activities, figuring out how to put the fires out can also be very challenging.

Some of the GMs in this study were responsible for operations that spanned the entire globe. Some were responsible for the manufacturing and selling of hundreds of different kinds of products. Some were responsible for operations that employed many different technologies. In the case of a typical GM, thousands of people, most of whom were not physically located close to him, were somehow involved in his operations on a daily basis. Under these circumstances, simply trying to monitor daily or weekly operational activity can be extremely difficult. The most impressive information-systems technology available today cannot monitor all this activity quickly and accurately. Even if it could, a GM could spend twenty-four hours a day simply trying to digest that information. Furthermore, under these circumstances, the sheer volume of relatively minor short-run problems can be enormous. B. J. Sparksman echoed the sentiments of many of the people in this study when he told me that "sometimes this job is just a never-ending supply of little problems."

Furthermore, the complex nature of the operational activities associated with most of these jobs can make it very difficult to know what to do when a "problem" is seen. During my visits with the GMs, I saw numerous instances of this. In one fairly typical case, the company involved was experiencing difficulty making shipments. The general manager, Richard Papolis, was faced with two questions: first, how important was this problem (and how much attention, if any, should he give to it); second, why was this happening (what was the underlying problem)? Papolis' subordinates had varying opinions regarding these questions. Some felt the problem was due to the poor performance of two individuals in manufacturing and could be corrected fairly easily. Others felt it was more complex, systemic, and important. They argued that the entire manufacturing function had not been keeping up with the company's growth. Still others felt the problem was caused mostly by the marketing department, which had been having trouble forecasting orders accurately. A few initial discussions on these issues brought Papolis a lot of information—both facts and opinions—but no clear answer to either of his questions. Such was often the case.

Again, to some degree, this kind of problem was a part of all the jobs in this study. Evidence from elsewhere also suggests that the same is probably true for most or all GMs.[4]

Job Demands II: Challenges and Dilemmas Associated
with the Relationships

In addition to responsibilities, the GM jobs placed the incumbents in a web of relationships which both influenced and were influenced by those responsibilities. Each major type of relationship usually created its own set of challenges and problems.

4. *Key Problem/Challenge #4: Getting the information, cooperation, and support needed from bosses to do the job. Being demanding with superiors without being perceived as uncooperative.* Like other managers, the GMs were not able to do their jobs without some support and cooperation from their superiors. Their bosses could supply critical resources, information, and rewards. Because of this, because their superiors were human (not "perfect" bosses), and for still other reasons, another important job challenge or problem related to managing relationships with a boss or a group of bosses.

Gerald Allen and Dan Donahue, both of whom were located a few levels below their corporate CEOs, had relatively weak and unrespected immediate bosses. In both cases, this made the task of reporting to top management and getting its support more difficult. Without extra effort on the parts of Allen and Donahue, messages from the top sometimes did not arrive clearly or on time, and their ideas or requests did not receive enough top-management attention. In addition, because their bosses could offer them so little, just dealing with them on a daily basis was often frustrating and took time away from more important matters.

Terry Franklin and Bob Anderson were physically located more than 1,000 miles from their bosses, and their businesses accounted for less than 10 percent of their bosses' responsibilities. Franklin only saw his boss two or three times a year. These factors gave Franklin and Anderson considerable daily autonomy but made it difficult to get their bosses' attention, understandably, or help.

Paul Jackson reported to a very strong corporate CEO who had once been his peer (and rival). Because their management styles were also very different, Jackson found dealing with his boss to be most difficult. Others in the company reported that his boss had reprimanded him loudly in public on a number of occasions. At one point, Jackson told me that, because of his boss, his job "simply was not any fun anymore."

Other GMs in the study had still other problems that made managing their relationships to their bosses difficult or frustrating or both. Even in those cases where it was not a "problem," the task of "managing up" was taken very seriously by the GMs. They all recognized that, to some degree, current job performance and future career success depended on it. Such appears to be the case not only in other GM jobs, but in most managerial jobs.[5]

5. *Key Problem/Challenge #5: Getting corporate staff, other relevant departments or divisions, and important external groups (e.g., big unions or customers or suppliers) to cooperate despite the lack of any formal authority over them; getting things done through them despite resistance, red tape, and the like.* Most of the GM jobs in this study had to interface with some corporate staff groups. Some also were required to coordinate functional groups that related to their businesses but that did not report directly to them. Still others had to deal with unions or other external groups because of their size and importance to the business. Many of these lateral relationships were somewhat adversarial in nature, and they often created problems for the GMs. Sometimes the problems were extensive.

When I asked Paul Jackson to tell me about the most difficult decision he had had to make in the past few years, he quickly replied that "making decisions is easy, but getting them implemented is sometimes nearly impossible. I have to work through so many people who do not report to me that it can be terribly difficult at times." John Thompson put it this way:

> This would be a much easier, and I think, more fun job if we were left alone to do our work. Instead, there are so many people that want to get into the act: corporate staff, other divisions, people from Washington, unions, etc., etc.

When I was visiting Jack Martin, he learned that actions made by two others in his corporation, neither of whom reported to him, would cost him about $350,000 on his bottom line. In neither case was he consulted or warned in advance; he was simply informed after the fact. And (obviously) he was furious! I watched Gerald Allen sit in the office of a staff manager (who did not report to him) for about thirty minutes while that manager was blatantly rude and offensive to him. But Allen sat calmly until he received assurances that something he needed would be done. In still other cases, I saw GMs struggle with corporate advertising departments who provided little service at a big cost, with important customers who wanted unreasonable favors, and with a wide variety of other similar situations.

Evidence from elsewhere suggests that these problems posed by lateral relationships are common today in general-management jobs, especially those in divisionalized firms.[6] Some evidence even suggests that they are a large part of most managerial jobs today.[7]

6. *Key Problem/Challenge #6: Motivating and controlling a large and diverse group of subordinates. Dealing with inadequate performance, interdepartmental conflict, and the like.* The general management jobs in this study gave the incumbents authority over what was usually a large and diverse yet interdependent group of people. The people typically had different points of view, different stakes in organizational decisions and outcomes, and sometimes quite different personalities. But the GMs had to depend upon them all, because they directly affected areas for which the GMs were responsible.

The GMs in this study often talked about motivating good performance, and nearly half said that the most difficult decision they had to make in the past few years was in regard to replacing a key subordinate. In each of these cases, the subordinate was not performing adequately, and the GM had to make difficult judgements regarding whether the person could ever improve, how much longer it might take, and the costs and risks of inadequate performance in the interim. I even watched Michael Richardson agonize over such a problem. In that situation, two of the key people reporting to one of his subordinates had recently quit, and some of those who remained were very upset about the way their boss was managing things. Richardson had already tried a few solutions to "the problem" that had not worked, yet he did not want to make an irreversible decision unless it was absolutely necessary. He had known this person for fifteen years and had put him in his current position. The whole situation was agonizing for the subordinate, for Richardson, and for those around him, some of whom were pressuring him to act in very different ways.

The GMs in this study also frequently commented about conflict and communication problems among subordinates and their departments. Bob Anderson told me that "The editorial side of the organization and the business side of the organization are two different worlds. Like oil and water, they don't mix well." Richard Poullin pointed out that "The creative people and the operating people would be at each other's throats in five minutes if we didn't constantly work to avoid these problems."

I witnessed a number of instances in which a GM had to become involved in a problem between subordinates from different departments. On some occasions, the conflicts were based on relatively simple misunderstandings. But in some cases, the problems were heated, very complex, and not at all easy to resolve. When I visited John Cohen, two of his young and ambitious subordinates were almost at each other's throats. Each sincerely believed the other person to be the source of conflict. One felt that the other was attacking him for political gain, the other saw the first as creating big problems for the company and refusing to listen to intelligent advice. After speaking to both of them, it was not at all obvious to me how to cool them off and resolve their differences without considerable effort.

Managing subordinates was a moderate-to-very-severe challenge in all the GM jobs in the study. Considerable evidence from elsewhere suggests that this is probably the norm for GM jobs, as well as for most other middle and upper level management jobs.[8]

The Overall Demands: A Summary

All of the demands associated with GM job responsibilities and relationships are summarized in Figures 2.1 and 2.2. Any one of the problems and challenges shown in these figures could make a job difficult. All six together add up to what can be a particularly stressful situation and a very difficult time-management problem. Many of the general managers in this study worked sixty or more hours a week, and some confided that the job could absorb 120 hours if they did not set some limits on themselves. Moreover, they usually worked in a rapid-pace, high-pressure environment. John Thompson, one of the GMs who had recently started in his first general-management role, expressed the problem this way:

> Before (in his previous job) it was easier to stop at 6:00, to turn off the job in my mind, and to go home. Now, even if I leave at 6:00, I find myself thinking or worrying about something on the way home and at home. There is always something.

Tom Long put it this way:

> It never ceases to amaze me how many people want to see me each day, and how many different problems they come up with. We could schedule meetings all day and all night if we didn't try to control it.

Of course, general-management jobs are not unique in the time they require or in the pressures involved. Other professional

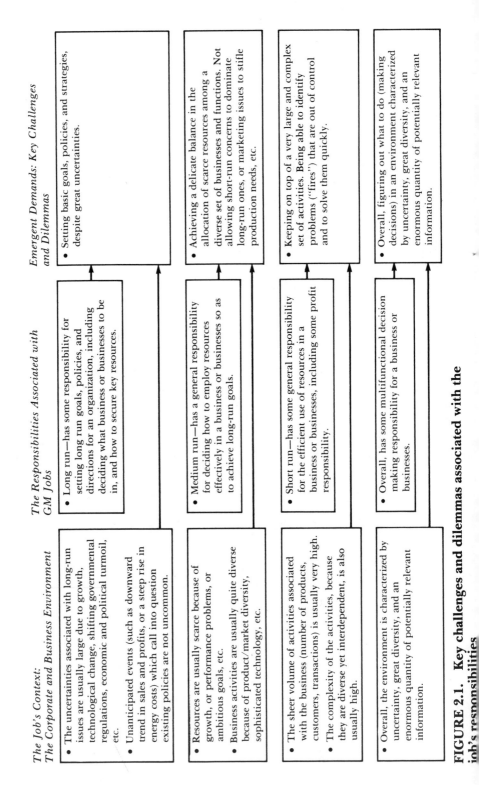

The Job's Context:
The Corporate and Business Environment

- The uncertainties associated with long-run issues are usually large due to growth, technological change, shifting governmental regulations, economic and political turmoil, etc.

- Unanticipated events (such as downward trend in sales and profits, or a steep rise in energy costs) which call into question existing policies are not uncommon.

- Resources are usually scarce because of growth, or performance problems, or ambitious goals, etc.

- Business activities are usually quite diverse because of product/market diversity, sophisticated technology, etc.

- The sheer volume of activities associated with the business (number of products, customers, transactions) is usually very high.

- The complexity of the activities, because they are diverse yet interdependent, is also usually high.

- Overall, the environment is characterized by uncertainty, great diversity, and an enormous quantity of potentially relevant information.

The Responsibilities Associated with GM Jobs

- Long run—has some responsibility for setting long run goals, policies, and directions for an organization, including deciding what business or businesses to be in, and how to secure key resources.

- Medium run—has a general responsibility for deciding how to employ resources effectively in a business or businesses so as to achieve long-run goals.

- Short run—has some general responsibility for the efficient use of resources in a business or businesses, including some profit responsibility.

- Overall, has some multifunctional decision making responsibility for a business or businesses.

Emergent Demands: Key Challenges and Dilemmas

- Setting basic goals, policies, and strategies, despite great uncertainties.

- Achieving a delicate balance in the allocation of scarce resources among a diverse set of businesses and functions. Not allowing short-run concerns to dominate long-run ones, or marketing issues to stifle production needs, etc.

- Keeping on top of a very large and complex set of activities. Being able to identify problems ("fires") that are out of control and to solve them quickly.

- Overall, figuring out what to do (making decisions) in an environment characterized by uncertainty, great diversity, and an enormous quantity of potentially relevant information.

FIGURE 2.1. Key challenges and dilemmas associated with the job's responsibilities

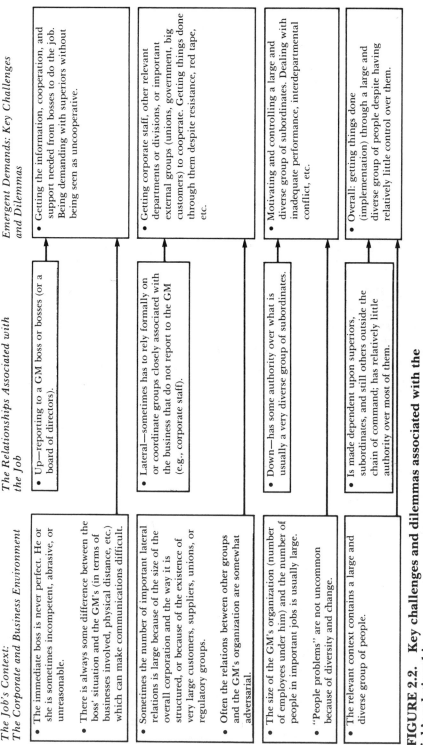

The Job's Context:
The Corporate and Business Environment

- The immediate boss is never perfect. He or she is sometimes incompetent, abrasive, or unreasonable.

- There is always some difference between the boss' situation and the GM's (in terms of businesses involved, physical distance, etc.) which can make communications difficult.

- Sometimes the number of important lateral relations is large because of the size of the overall corporation and the way it is structured, or because of the existence of very large customers, suppliers, unions, or regulatory groups.

- Often the relations between other groups and the GM's organization are somewhat adversarial.

- The size of the GM's organization (number of employees under him) and the number of people in important jobs is usually large.

- "People problems" are not uncommon because of diversity and change.

- The relevant context contains a large and diverse group of people.

The Relationships Associated with the Job

- Up—reporting to a GM boss or bosses (or a board of directors).

- Lateral—sometimes has to rely formally on or coordinate groups closely associated with the business that do not report to the GM (e.g., corporate staff).

- Down—has some authority over what is usually a very diverse group of subordinates.

- Is made dependent upon superiors, subordinates, and still others outside the chain of command; has relatively little authority over most of them.

Emergent Demands: Key Challenges and Dilemmas

- Getting the information, cooperation, and support needed from bosses to do the job. Being demanding with superiors without being seen as uncooperative.

- Getting corporate staff, other relevant departments or divisions, or important external groups (unions, government, big customers) to cooperate. Getting things done through them despite resistance, red tape, etc.

- Motivating and controlling a large and diverse group of subordinates. Dealing with inadequate performance, interdepartmental conflict, etc.

- Overall: getting things done (implementation) through a large and diverse group of people despite having relatively little control over them.

FIGURE 2.2. Key challenges and dilemmas associated with the job's relationships

and managerial jobs can be very time-consuming and stressful. Nor can the demands listed in Figures 2.1 and 2.2 be found only in GM jobs. To a degree, almost all management jobs have somewhat similar demands; but general-management jobs seem to be unique with respect to the overall diversity of demands.

No other managerial or professional job places a person in a position where he or she must deal with long-, medium-, and short-run tasks, as well as with a very diverse group of specialists in a variety of different kinds of relationships. All other jobs somehow limit the diversity of demands. For example, lower-level management jobs do not have the long-run responsibilities. Other higher-level management jobs do not have the same variety of specialists as subordinates. Staff jobs and traditional professional jobs seldom have many subordinates at all. Only GM jobs contain all this task- and people-related diversity. Ultimately, therefore, it is the *diversity* of complex demands that makes the job a *general* management job, that makes it different, and that makes it particularly difficult.

Differences in Job Demands

Although the GM jobs in this study shared the same six basic demands, there was considerable variation among them in terms of the overall intensity of those demands, the relative importance of the six problem areas, and the exact nature of each demand. For example, although all of the GM jobs in this study presented the incumbent with difficult decision-making problems, figuring out what to do was much more complex in some settings than others. Likewise, although all the jobs contained difficult implementation problems, getting things done was clearly much more demanding in some situations than in others.

In general, it appears that at least two major factors help create these kinds of differences associated with GM jobs (see Figure 2.3). First of all, differences in the job itself appear to be important. There seem to be a number of different kinds of GM jobs that are common today, each of which has a slightly different configuration of responsibilities and relationships. Second, differences in the business and corporate contexts seem to be very important. Running a banking business, for example, can present very different problems from running an automobile parts business. And running that business in a small, young, western com-

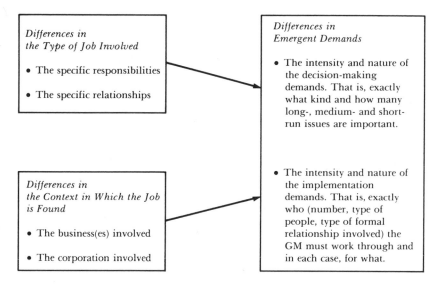

FIGURE 2.3.   Factors that create differences in GM job demands

pany can present very different problems from running it in a large, old, eastern corporation.[9]

Seven Different Kinds of GM Jobs

Before World War I, for all practical purposes there was only one type of GM job in the United States: a chief executive officer (CEO) reporting to a board of directors, with full responsibility for a functionally organized company. Even up to World War II, probably 95 percent or more of all GM jobs were of this single type. But in the past forty years, as businesses have grown larger, more diverse, and more complex, different kinds of GM jobs have emerged in some significant number. These jobs have been "invented" along with more and more complex organizational structures to help corporations manage their large size and diversity.[10] Today there are at least seven different, commonly found types of GM jobs. These include what I will call the functional CEO; the multidivisional CEO; the group GM; the autonomous division GM; the semiautonomous division GM; the product/market GM; and the operations GM. Briefly, the seven types can be described as follows:

1. CEO in a functionally organized company: This is the "tra-

ditional" GM job, which reports to a board of directors (or chairman) and has functional managers reporting to it.

2. Corporate CEO in a multidivisional company: The most obvious difference between this and the first type is that general managers, in addition to some staff functional managers, report to this position. Furthermore, the multidivisional CEO usually has fewer short-run responsibilities.

3. Group GM: This type of GM job reports to a general manager and has GMs reporting to him. A typical group GM, for example, might report to a multidivisional CEO and have six or seven division GMs reporting to him. This job also tends to have fewer long-run responsibilities than a CEO and fewer important external lateral relations (e.g., to bankers).

4. Autonomous division GM: This type of GM is in many ways like the traditional job (#1), except that it reports to a GM, not a chairman or a board of directors. Like the group GM, it tends to have fewer long-run responsibilities than a CEO, more short-run responsibilities, and fewer corporate external lateral relations. Often the key responsibility in this job is for profit.

5. Semiautonomous division GM: This GM job is like the last, except that it has fewer downward but more internal lateral relations (to corporate staff), it reports more closely upwards, and it tends to have slightly fewer responsibilities overall. For example, a typical semiautonomous division GM might report to a Group GM (who has several other divisions with related products/services/markets) and have to rely to some degree on corporate (or group-level) personnel, legal, accounting, public relations, and financial staff.

6. Product/market GM: This type of general manager tends to have even fewer types of subordinates and more lateral relations. Typically, for example, mostly marketing people will report to this job, but the GM will be responsible for coordinating the manufacturing and engineering people associated with his business (or businesses). This job also has still fewer long-run responsibilities.

7. Operations GM: This final type of common GM job tends to have the least overall long-run and the most short-run responsibility. It tends to have mostly manufacturing or sales/service personnel reporting to it and to have some lateral relations (which, unlike the P/M GM, it does not have to coordinate closely). A typical operations GM might be the manager of a plant or a

group of plants who is only partially responsible for a calculated "profit," and who has some personnel, accounting, and other staff reporting to him.

Of these seven types, the functional CEO, autonomous division GM, and the operations GM are probably the most common in existence today. The multidivisional CEO and group GM are probably the rarest (accounting for only about 1 percent of the total). For example, there are probably fewer than 1500 group GMs in the U.S.[11] There are undoubtedly even more types of GM jobs that are even rarer and less visible today (such as, for example, "Sector" GMs) or are slightly different from the seven types described here.

Of the GMs in this study, two were operations GMs (Allen and Long); four were product/market GMs (Gaines, Martin, Jackson, and Donahue); three were semiautonomous division GMs (Poullin, Thompson, and Sparksman); five were autonomous division GMs (Anderson, Cohen, Franklin, Firono, and Papolis); one was a functional CEO (Richardson); and none was a group GM or mutidivisional CEO GM. The absence of the latter two types was purposive, although in retrospect it was a mistake. (When designing the study I was warned not to include GMs who were managers of GMs because those jobs may be "different." Implicitly, the assumption was that there may be two types of GM jobs.)

Some people might argue that only the first four types of GM jobs are *really* GM jobs (or perhaps just #1, #2, and #4, or even just #1 and #4). In doing so, they implicitly apply a relationship-oriented criterion in defining the job. For example, the most common restrictive definition assumes that all GM jobs, like the traditional one, should have no lateral relationships of any consequence inside the firm and always have all relevant functions reporting to them. But such a definition misses, I think, the core of the job, which is responsibility-oriented. All of the seven types of GM jobs identified here have some multifunctional responsibility for a business or businesses; that is the real essence of a GM job.

One of the giant corporations in this study had six of the seven types of GM jobs within its structure. Figure 2.4 shows in a rough way how these six types of GM jobs were different yet related in this one setting. The corporate CEO job in that corporation was unique in that it had long-run responsibilities that were much more demanding than its short-run responsibilities. The operations GM job stands out for the opposite reason; it had short-run responsibilities that were much more demanding than its long-run ones. The product/market GM job was most different because it had the greatest lateral relationship demands. And the group GM job stands out because, when the incumbents had autonomous division GMs reporting to them, they were in the unusual position of having both a boss and a subordinate who had more autonomy (in a lateral sense) than they did (which did not make the group GMs very comfortable).

The overall pattern in Figure 2.4 is that as one moves down the hierarchy in a very large corporation, GM jobs tend to be less

FIGURE 2.4.   Differences in job demands among six types of GM jobs in one corporation

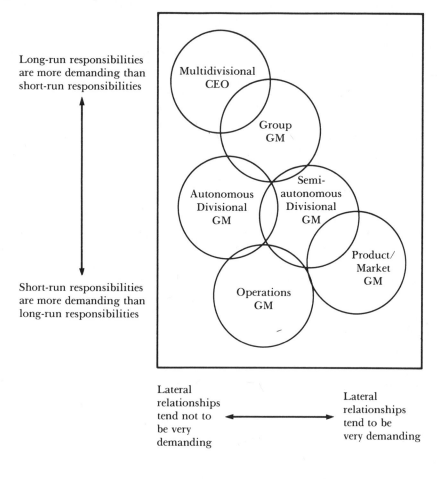

demanding on long-run issues and more demanding on both short-run issues and lateral relations. Given the nature of modern organization structures, this is not surprising.

Different Business and Corporate Settings: The Impact of Size, Age, Performance Level, and Other Factors

Although significant differences in job demands were created by differences in the type of GM job involved, even more and larger variations resulted from differences in the business and corporate contexts. This is so because while there seem to be roughly seven different types of GM jobs today, variations in numerous dimensions make for dozens of different types of business and corporate contexts. These dimensions included such things as: the growth rate of the business; the rate of technological change; the level of profitability (or loss); the ambitiousness of top management; the diversity of products and markets; the sheer number of products and yearly volume; the nature of the GM's immediate boss; the way the overall firm is structured; the number of employees involved in the business; the types of people involved; the maturity of the products and markets; the number (if any) of very large customers or suppliers or unions or regulators; the degree to which businesses and functions are interdependent; and the nature of the organization's culture. Of these factors, three seem to be particularly important: size, age, and performance level.

Some of the contexts in this study were much larger than others. Paul Jackson was responsible for a multibillion dollar business in which tens of thousands of people were involved. Michael Richardson was responsible for only a few million dollars of business in which only a few hundred people were involved. These size differences appear to be very important in making job demands different in different settings.

To some degree, the relationship here is very straightforward; the GM jobs associated with larger businesses and larger organizations tended to be "bigger" jobs. That is, they tended to be more demanding overall than were jobs in smaller contexts. For example, in large contexts like Gaines' or Jackson's, the job responsibilities were made more complex by the sheer volume of issues, decisions, and activities; hence decision making was more difficult. Furthermore, job-related relationships were usually much more numerous, and getting things done through others much more difficult.

But at the same time, size also made job demands different in some qualitatively important ways. First of all, job demands in large and small contexts were different because of differences in the informational environment. In the large settings, the GMs could seldom get as much detailed information for decision making as one could get in the small settings. To a degree, this changed the nature and the problems associated with decision making. For example, in a small setting such as Anderson's or Richardson's, the GMs could often monitor daily operations visually and intervene directly to get information. In large settings this was rarely possible, often because facilities were geographically dispersed. In a smaller setting, the GM could often approach resource-allocation decisions with a very detailed knowledge of all the issues involved. Again, this was rarely possible in the large settings, and that changed the nature of the resource-allocation problem.

To an even greater degree, the job demands in large contexts and small contexts were qualitatively different because of the human environment. In large contexts, the GMs tended to have to work through much more elaborate and bureaucratic structures and systems. For example, in the large settings, the "managing-up" demand was often different from that in small settings because the boss was physically located somewhere else and because there were formal planning and control systems that affected their relationships. Managing laterally was often different because there were usually more specialist staff groups in existence and because informal relationships among line and staff groups were often more adversarial. The managing-down demand was often different because, unlike in the small settings, one simply could not deal with everyone on a face-to-face, one-to-one basis; there were just too many people. Managing-down problems were also different in a large setting because of the bureaucracy (the rules and procedures and formal systems) that usually existed.

Some of the contexts in the study had much more mature products and markets than others. For example, the GMs in the two banking businesses (Allen and Thompson) were working with products and markets that, for all practical purposes, were over fifty years old. But one GM in a high-technology industry (Papolis) was working with products and markets less than a decade old. These differences in product/market maturity do not seem to produce differences in job demands that are as dramatic or straightforword as differences in size, but age differences do seem to be very important.

First of all, the information- and decision-making environment in older contexts was more standardized and routine. After years of experience with a product and a group of customers, potential new directions for the business, resource-allocation alternatives, and potential operational control problems were often well known. As such, the overall level of uncertainty was lower. These businesses were generally less turbulent, usually because they were not growing very fast. All of this affected the decision-making demands.

Furthermore, the human environment was usually different, too. In older contexts, I often found an older workforce, one that tended to think of itself as professionals or craftsmen (for example, bankers or tire makers). They tended to have relatively strong beliefs about right and wrong ways to do their jobs. Obviously, these factors all affected relationship or implementation demands.

Some of the businesses and corporations in the study were performing much better than others. For example, when Bob Anderson, Richard Poullin, and Dan Donahue stepped into their jobs, their divisions were all losing money. They were put in to "turn things around." But when Tom Long and John Thompson started their jobs, their businesses were doing quite well. Their predecessors had been promoted for just that reason.

Such differences in profitability affected GM job demands in a number of ways. In low-performing contexts, decision-making demands tended to be more difficult for two basic reasons: first, there were more decisions to be made. When things were going well, the GMs did not have to aggressively consider new directions for their businesses or new ways of allocating resources. When performance was low, others obviously did. Second, the speed with which decisions had to be made was higher in the low-performing contexts. GMs in high-performing contexts could relax to some degree, but those in turnaround situations had to move quickly before the firm "died."

Performance differences also seem to affect the relationships or people demands. In the "turnaround" contexts, the GMs found themselves more dependent on people simply because more had to be done by others to change things. And they usually found themselves with at least some subordinates who were performing very poorly. Dealing with this latter problem often tended to be a major demand for Donahue, Poullin, and Anderson in their first few months on the job.

A variety of other contextual differences also created differences in job demands, although less dramatically than those just described. For example, the diversity of products and markets associated with the job seems to be important. In the more diverse contexts, it was much more difficult to comprehend all the details associated with the products and markets; it was also more difficult to relate to what was often a more diverse set of people. In those contexts with more political and economic turmoil, the uncertainty associated with decision making was higher, and the decision-making demands more difficult. In those contexts with a "difficult" immediate boss, the managing-up task was obviously more difficult. And so on.

All of these factors, and their effects on GM job demands, were implicit in Figures 2.1 and 2.2. These relationships are summarized in a more explicit way in Figure 2.5.

Although relatively little research has focused on differences among managerial (especially executive) jobs,[12] that which has is consistent with our findings here.[13] So is the extensive organizational research from the past two decades which has focused on identifying key variables that cause variations within organizations.[14]

Summary and Discussion

Two characteristics of the GM jobs in this study are particularly striking. First they were, on the average, extremely demanding in terms of both decision making and implementation. Informational contexts, characterized by major uncertainties, great diversity, and high volume—in combination with human contexts, characterized by large numbers of people, diverse orientations, and dependent relationships—almost always posed serious intellectual and interpersonal problems for the incumbents. Furthermore a casual look at basic business trends suggests that

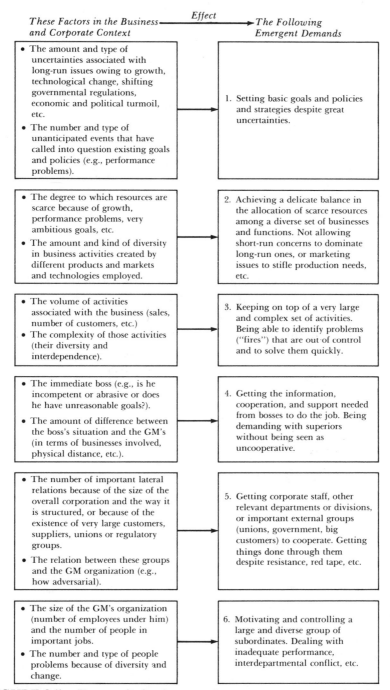

FIGURE 2.5.   Factors in business and corporate contexts that help create differences in GM job demands in different settings

not only are these jobs very demanding, they are becoming increasingly so (see Figure 2.6). Corporate diversification and growth, technological developments, governmental regulation, and international competition all conspire to make the demands associated with GM job responsibilities more complex. At the same time, changing worker attitudes to authority figures, the increasing heterogeneity of the workforce, the increasing size of the workforce, and the increasing education level of the typical employee all make the demands associated with GM job relationships more difficult to manage. Of course, to some degree, these same trends are making all management jobs more difficult. But at the general management level, I suspect they are making very difficult jobs into ones that are potentially—at least in a few cases —impossible.

Second, the fifteen GM jobs in this study were different in many ways. Despite sharing some "core" similarities, the jobs varied considerably in terms of the demands they placed on the incumbents. This variation seems to be caused by differences in the type of GM job, the businesses involved, and the corporations involved. The patterns of differences identified here are important for a number of reasons. As new types of GM jobs have emerged over the past few decades, and as the diversity of organizational size and product/market age have increased, the differences among GM jobs have undoubtedly been growing. They will

FIGURE 2.6. Basic business trends and their effect on the demands associated with general management jobs

Trends	*Effect on Demands*
Corporate diversification Corporate growth New technological developments Governmental regulation International competition	Associated with the job responsibilities: short-, medium-, and long-run tasks are becoming more complex.
Changing worker attitude toward authority figures Increasing heterogeneity in the workforce More people owing to growth Increasing education level in the workforce	Associated with the job relationships: relationships with bosses, peers, and subordinates are becoming more difficult to manage.

probably continue to grow in the future. As such, the effects of these patterns will also grow. And, as we shall see next, these patterns are related to differences in the characteristics of effective GMs.

3

The General Managers: Personal and Background Characteristics

ONE THINKS OF general managers, obviously, as generalists. So do they. Most of the GMs in this study felt that they could do a pretty good job managing or advising nearly any organization: another division in their company, another company, a state or federal department, even a business school. Not that they were interested in doing so; most were quite satisfied with their current jobs. But they felt that they and other really good managers could do so if they wanted. The underlying belief here—that a really well prepared and competent "professional" manager can manage nearly anything—is probably shared by many others also, including some business-school academics. Nevertheless, the data from this study strongly suggest that this belief is almost entirely wrong.

Almost all of the GMs in this study were highly *specialized*. That is, they had personal characteristics that closely fit the specific demands of the contexts in which they worked. Because those demands were in some ways similar across all fifteen situations and yet were different in other ways, the GMs were also in some ways very similar and in other ways quite different. The process of specialization which created those similarities and differences started nearly at birth and continued right up until the time of the study. In it, the GMs specialized in business, in management, in a particular industry, in a particular company, and in the general management function itself. As we will see in this and subsequent chapters, such specialization seems to have been central to their ability to cope with the often huge demands placed upon them by their jobs.

To explore this pattern of specialization, we will begin by looking at personal characteristics shared by the GMs. We will then focus on shared background characteristics, and finally on differences in personal and background characteristics.

Common Personal Characteristics

The fifteen individuals in this study were chosen because they held and were believed to be performing well in general-management jobs. No personal or background characteristics were considered per se, except to make sure that we did not inadvertently get some obviously odd distribution of those characteristics (such as only people under forty-five years old, or only people educated in one state). We did not, even without any active intervention on my part.

In looking at this group of people, one is at first glance struck by the great diversity. They are tall and short, young and old, conservative and liberal, mellow and stern, northern and southern. They certainly do not seem to fit into any simple mold. But when one looks closer and deeper, a large number of similarities also emerge. Indeed, there are more than a dozen different personal characteristics which seem to have been shared by most or all of the GMs in this study (see Figure 3.1). Most relate to elements of basic personality—needs/motives, temperament, cognitive orientation, and interpersonal orientation. The rest relate to information and relationships that had been accumulated or developed in adulthood.

Basic Personality

In terms of basic personality, the themes that seem to run through the data on the GMs relate to power, achievement, ambition, emotional stability, optimism, intelligence, analytical ability, intuition, a personable style, and an ability to relate easily to a broad set of business specialists.[1]

BASIC PERSONALITY

Needs/Motives

—Liked power

—Liked achievement

—Ambitious

Temperament

—Emotionally stable and even

—Optimistic

Cognitive Orientation

—Above average intelligence (but not brilliant)

—Moderately strong analytically

—Strong intuitively

Interpersonal Orientation

—Personable, and good at developing relationships with people

—Unusual set of interests that allowed them to relate easily to a broad set of business specialists

ACCUMULATED INFORMATION AND RELATIONSHIPS

Information

—Very knowledgeable about their businesses

—Very knowledgeable about their organizations

Relationships

—Had cooperative relationships with a very large number of people in their organizations

—Had cooperative relations with many people in their industry also

FIGURE 3.1.   Shared personal characteristics

All except one or possibly two of the GMs seem to have been strongly achievement oriented. When asked about "high points" in their lives, one of their two most common responses involved achieving business results. As Dan Donahue put it, "We went from a $1 million loss last year to a $3.5 million profit this year. One gets a feeling of accomplishment from that." This same need for achievement can also be seen in their responses to a question about job satisfaction. By and large, they were all satisfied with their jobs, but the ones that were performing better were more satisified.[2] Furthermore, this achievement need was often observed by others. In a typical example, one of Michael Richardson's subordinates told me that Richardson so liked to win and be the best that he "probably wants very much to be the best GM in your study."

With only one exception, the GMs also seem to have liked status and power a great deal. For example, the second most common response to the question regarding "high points" in their lives related to a recent promotion. Most of them obviously enjoyed taking on a position with considerable status and power in their firms. Furthermore, as others noted and I observed, the GMs seemed to have been relatively unconflicted in using or dealing with power. Chuck Gaines is a good example in this regard. "When I was in charge of the Firebrand subsidiary two years ago," he told me, "I learned that one of our products had a potential safety problem. It quickly became clear to me that we should recall the product. From a moral point of view, from a long term point of view, this was very clear. But a lot of people didn't want to deal with the immediate consequences. And there were many immediate consequences. Our quarterly earnings would disappear. Some of our dealers would be very upset. Product development and manufacturing people would be on the defensive. Let me tell you, the pressure was strong not to do the recall." Yet he did so, without hesitation or any visible sense of doubt.

Related to the two previous points, most of the GMs seem to have been highly motivated and ambitious. Despite the fact that they already had high-level jobs and very good pay, most still wanted more responsibility, power, and income. Some, like Tom Long and Richard Poullin, wanted to be one of the two or three people who ran their very large corporations. Others, like Dan Donahue, Gerald Allen, and Richard Papolis did not want to be corporate CEOs, but wanted to play much larger roles in shaping the future of their companies. And virtually everyone wanted more money and measured his career success by his income relative to other executives his age. Indeed, their satisfaction with their careers related very closely with how much money they were making relative to others their own ages.[3]

In terms of temperament, almost all of them seem to have been very stable emotionally.[4] This was observable, and others frequently commented on this trait. One of Richard Poullin's subordinates put it this way: "When everybody else around here is bouncing off the walls, Richard is still as calm as ever. He doesn't go through manic-depressive cycles like some of us." I saw numerous instances of this while with Poullin and others; some were quite striking. On one occasion, for example, when one of John Cohen's subordinates burst into his office nearly hysterical, Cohen simply looked at the man with calm eyes, and with his usual steady voice said: "Sit down Fred and tell me all about it."

Temperamentally, most of the GMs also seem to have been very optimistic. When others could see nothing but gloom on the horizon, the GMs could always see some opportunities or some positive signs. This was quite visible and was often commented upon by them (sometimes as a criticism of the GMs).

Interpersonally, all of the GMs were both personable and good at developing relationships with people (although some more so than others). Again, this was easy to observe and was often commented on by others. Paul Jackson was one of the best in this regard. After being with him only sixty minutes on our first meeting, I felt as if he were almost an old friend. It came as no surprise later when one of his subordinates told me that "almost everyone around here is very fond of Paul."

Also in terms of interpersonal orientation, most of the GMs had an identifiable response pattern on the Strong-Campbell Interest Inventory.[5] This pattern suggests an unusual ability to relate to a diverse group of business specialists. For example, in the case of Tom Long, the test showed high scores (above 40) in four sales/marketing-oriented occupations, three operations-oriented occupations, two financial occupations, three external-relations occupations, the legal function, and the personnel function.[6]

Cognitively, all of the GMs seemed to be above average in intelligence. I say "seemed" because I did not have them take any standard intelligence test; this conclusion is based on interviews with others. But only two of the fifteen were seen by others as "very intelligent" people—that is, people who score over 140 on traditional intelligence tests. For example, in the most typical case, of the ten people I interviewed who worked with the GM, over half described the person as "smart" or "intelligent." Only in two cases did no one mention intelligence, and in only five cases did most people use a stronger description (e.g., brilliant, very intelligent).

In terms of cognitive skills, most of the GMs appear to have been reasonably strong both analytically and intuitively. That is, they seem to have been able to think systematically, deductively, and inductively. But they also had a highly developed "gut feel." Once again, people regularly commented about these qualities during my interviews. The most common terms they used in this respect to describe the GMs were "having good judgement," "analytically strong," "systematic in his thinking," "good at spotting problems," and "logical."

Knowledge and Relationships

In addition to sharing a number of personality characteristics, the GMs also tended to be very similar in terms of certain aspects of business knowledge and business relationships. Specifically, they were all very knowledgeable about the businesses they were in, and they all had an extensive set of relationships with people throughout their companies and often throughout their industries.

Although some were clearly more knowledgeable than others, the typical GM was an "expert" in his business. He knew a great deal about the specific products, competitors, markets, customers, technologies, unions, and government regulations associated with his industry. In addition, all were very knowledgeable about their companies. The typical GM knew an enormous amount about different people, organizational procedures, the history of the company, specific products, and so on.

It is difficult to convey just how much tangible business-related detail the typical GM had; I certainly do not have any good measure of this. But from listening and talking to them, it was very clear to me that I could have interviewed them for weeks, if not months or years, and still not tapped all the detail. That is, the GMs seemed to possess encyclopedic detail on their businesses and corporations.[7]

In addition, the typical GM had a set of cooperative relationships in his firm and industry which included hundreds of people; at the extreme, even thousands were involved. This included bosses, peers, and subordinates inside the corporation as well as customers, suppliers, union officials, competitors, and government people outside the firm.

For example, Jack Martin was alleged by those who worked with him personally to know well over a thousand people in his company and industry. In varying degrees, these people either liked him, respected him, felt they owed him something, or simply felt he was an important person. As one of these people told me: "I'm not sure I have even met as many people as he knows on a first-name basis."

Some of the GMs in the study had even more cooperative business relationships than did Martin. Most had fewer. But all had, by any reasonable standard, a lot.

Job-related Reasons for the Similarities

In total, the GMs in this study appear to have shared over a dozen different personal characteristics. In terms of motivation, temperament, cognitive orientation, interpersonal orientation, information, and relationships, they were remarkably similar in many ways.

Although few prior studies have focused on the personal characteristics of GMs, some evidence does exist which suggests that the items in Figure 3.1 are not idiosyncratic to this group of fifteen people, especially the personality characteristics.[8] Nevertheless, one might reasonably wonder whether a different group of GMs would have led to a different list, or whether these characteristics really differentiate GMs from other managers (or from people in general.) Without a great deal more data, we cannot address these concerns completely. But we can inquire as to whether there are any logical job-related reasons why we may have found this particular list of similarities.

In Chapter 2, we saw that the GM job tends to present the incumbent with a number of difficult challenges and problems which, taken together, can be very demanding in both an interpersonal and an intellectual sense. On the one hand, the job makes the GM responsible for a large, complex, and diverse set of interdependent activities. Under these circumstances, figuring out what to do (making decisions) can be very difficult because of the uncertainty, the diversity, and the enormous quantity of potentially relevant information. At the same time, the job also makes the GM dependent on superiors, a large and very diverse group of subordinates, and still others outside his chain of command. As such, getting things implemented can also be extremely difficult. A careful examination of Figure 3.1 suggests that virtually all of these shared personal characteristics might be very helpful (if not essential) under these difficult circumstances (see Figure 3.2).

Extensive knowledge of the business and the organization for which one is responsible may well be essential for effective managerial decision making under conditions of great complexity. Such knowledge can help guide one in sorting through enormous quantities of potentially relevant information and then in making sense of that information. Under relatively simple conditions, common sense can serve as a guide, and/or the relevant knowledge can be learned in a short period of time. Neither is probably possible under conditions of great complexity.

Likewise, the cognitive characteristics of above average intelligence, analytical ability, and intuitive ability are undoubtedly very helpful in complex situations. They give one the ability to gather, store, and manipulate large amounts of complex information. In a similar way, the temperamental characteristic of optimism and the motivational characteristic of wanting to achieve might give one the desire to use those skills in a complex and difficult GM job. Both the ability and the drive would seem to be needed.

Having extensive informal relationships throughout the organization (and industry) should help enormously in getting things done, in getting decisions implemented, under conditions of great dependency. These relationships can help mobilize people and resources over which one has little formal control. In circumstances where one is not made very dependent on others by the job, such relationships are much less valuable; one can implement things by doing them oneself.

Likewise, the interpersonal characteristics of a personable style, skill at developing relationships, and an ability to relate to a diverse group of business sepcialists should all be very helpful under conditions of high dependence on a diverse group of people. They would seem to give one the ability to develop, maintain, and use relationships with relevant others. In concert with this, the motivational characteristic of liking power and the temperamental characteristic of being emotionally even should give one the inclination to want to use those abilities in a GM job situation.

Finally, being very ambitious might be important in attracting people to jobs that can provide considerable income and status,

The GM Jobs

Key Demands

Responsibilities and Relationships

- Is responsible for a large, complex, and very diverse set of inter-dependent activities.

- Is dependent on superiors, a large and very diverse set of subordinates, and still others outside the chain of command.

Emergent Demands

- Figuring out what to do (making decisions) in an environment characterized by uncertainty, great diversity, and an enormous quantity of potentially relevant information.

- Getting things done through a large and diverse set of people (including bosses, subordinates and others) despite having little direct control over most of them.

Overall: An extremely demanding job, but one that provides status and income.

The GMs

Personal Characteristics

Accumulated Information and Relationships

- Very knowledgeable about both their businesses and their organizations.

- Have extensive relationships throughout their organizations (and their industries).

Basic Personality

- Above-average intelligence, good analytical and intuitive skills, optimistic, and achievement oriented.

- Personable, like power, good at developing relationships, emotionally even, and have an unusual ability to relate to diverse groups of business specialists.

- Very ambitious.

FIGURE 3.2. Shared personal characteristics and their relationships to key GM job demands

and in keeping them there despite the great pressures, demands, and problems.

In other words, the reason that the GMs shared the personal characteristics delineated in Figure 3.1 is probably because their jobs were alike in a number of core ways that required most or all of those characteristics. Those characteristics give a person both the ability and the inclination to deal with the difficult decision-making and implementation issues associated with the job. In a sense, these characteristics seem to fit the key aspects of the job (see Figure 3.2) in ways that allow a person both to survive and to prosper despite the very difficult job demands.

Furthermore, since all of the GMs were performing fairly well, one obvious interpretation of this finding is that individual job "fit" is related to performance. A closer look at the data clearly supports this interpretation.

Some of the GMs in this study were performing at a level one might call "excellent," others at a "very good" level, and still others at a "good to fair" level (see Appendix E). In examining these differences, one can find a pattern which relates to individual job fit. Specifically, the better performers started their current GM jobs with characteristics that seem to have better fit the specific demands connected with those jobs. They had knowledge of their businesses and organizations as well as native intelligence which better fit the complexity of the tasks and activities associated with their jobs. They also had interpersonal skills and relationships with relevant others which better fit the people dependencies inherent in their jobs.

It appears that the better "fit" in the cases of the higher performers was the result of both stronger personal characteristics on the part of those GMs and, to some degree, less demanding jobs (especially relationally demanding). For example, both the excellent performers were described by others as very skilled in dealing with people (e.g., personable and good at developing relationships). Most of the very good performers were also described this way, but only one of the three good/fair performers was. Both excellent performers were also described by others as very intelligent and having very good judgement. Most of the very good performers were thus described, but only one of the three fair/good performers was. In terms of job demands, when both excellent performers started their jobs, they had fewer than 400 people under them in their organizations. Again, this was

true for most of the very good performers, but for only one of
the three good/fair performers. Furthermore, neither of the excellent performers had an operations or product/market GM job
(and the associated lateral demands), but half the very good performers did, and most of the good/fair performers did.

It would thus appear that a person may need both a large
number of personal assets (Figure 3.1) and a "manageable" job in
order to perform at an excellent level in a GM job. Having only
good business judgement," or great interpersonal skills, or a lot
of ambition is not enough. One needs a number of different
motivational, temperamental, interpersonal, cognitive, informational, and relational characteristics.[9] It is the total set of personal
assets, and how well they fit the job demands, that is important.

Common Background Characteristics

In addition to personal characteristics, the GMs in the study
shared a significant number of common background characteristics (see Figure 3.3). They grew up in family environments which
were alike in many ways; they also shared a number of common
educational and career experiences.

It is conceivable that these common background characteristics occur by chance, but that is unlikely. Later in the chapter we
will argue that it is more probable that we have found the pattern
shown in Figure 3.3 because those experiences were central in
shaping the common personal characteristics that we have just
discussed.

Childhood Family Environment

Most of the GMs had an upwardly mobile set of parents. They
typically had lower-middle-class or middle-class grandparents and
middle-class or upper-middle-class parents.

All but two grew up with both original parents at home and
report having had close relationships with those parents. Frank
Firono was fairly typical in this regard; he spoke with true affec-
tion about his parents, especially his mother, whom he described
as "one of the warmest people I have ever met." When I asked
Frank about major people or events that had influenced his ca-

---

<u>CHILDHOOD FAMILY ENVIRONMENT</u>

- Upwardly mobile parents
- Both original parents at home while growing up
- Close relationship with one or both parents
- At least one parent with two- or four-year college education
- Fathers associated with business and/or working as managers in nonbusiness setting
- Brothers and sisters (no only children)

<u>EDUCATIONAL EXPERIENCES</u>

- An undergraduate or graduate (master's) education
- Business-related degrees
- Student leaders in high school, college, or both

<u>EARLY CAREER EXPERIENCES</u>

- Joined (or started) a firm (or industry) that closely fit personal interests and values
- Spent the vast majority of career time in that one industry
- Spent the vast majority of career time with current employer
- Rose through one function (or two at the most)
- Rapidly promoted
- Promoted into first general-management job early in career (between the ages of thirty-four and forty)

FIGURE 3.3. Shared background characteristics

reer, he immediately began to talk about the quality of his relationship with his parents: "They had high expectations and they gave me a lot of support."

Almost all of them had at least one parent with a college education (four or two years), but only two of the fathers had a graduate degree. In one typical case, Richard Poullin's father had a BS degree and his mother had two years of junior college. Most of the GMs had fathers who were associated with business as managers or salesmen. One of the other fathers was a manager in the navy, one a rural mail carrier, one a farmer (and farm manager), one a medical professional, and one a lawyer.

None of the GMs was an only child. All had at least one sibling; four of the GMs had one, six had two, three had three, one had four, and one had five. Most were not the first-born child; four were actually the last born.

Educational and Career Experiences

All the GMs had at least an undergraduate education, although only three of them attended prestigious schools (Harvard, Yale, and Princeton). Most also had graduate degrees, usually MBAs. Almost all of the degrees were in business-related specialties such as business, economics, and engineering.

While in high school and college, almost all of the GMs were student leaders. Many were captains of sports teams, and some were the heads of clubs or of the student government. That is, almost all displayed an interest in leadership and management at a relatively early age. Bob Anderson was typical in this regard. In high school he was the editor of the yearbook and the president of two student clubs. In college he was a class officer and was voted outstanding freshman and senior by his fraternity.

After school, and sometimes after a period in the armed services or with one or two initial employers, most settled into an industry and a company rather quickly. Typically, they chose an environment which closely matched their interests and values. Once settled in, they stayed put. On the average, 90 percent of the time in their careers was spent in the industry in which they were engaged at the time of the study. Only one person spent most of his career in a different, though related, industry. On the average, 81 percent of the time in their careers was spent with their present employers. Only three spent more than half of their careers with employers other than their current ones. In other words, despite all we hear about executive mobility from company to company, these GMs were not at all mobile in an interorganizational sense; they specialized in a particular industry and in a particular company.

The GMs rose quickly in their organizations. Indeed, most

developed what might be called a "success syndrome." That is a pattern:

- where they did well in an early assignment;
- that led to a promotion, or a somewhat more challenging assignment;
- that reinforced (or even increased) their self-esteem and motivation and led to an increase in their formal or informal power and an increase in the opportunities available to develop more power. The more challenging jobs also stretched them and helped build their skills;
- that in turn led to an increase in their relevant relationships (including one or more with a mentor in top management), an increase in their relevant knowledge, and an increase in their interpersonal and intellectual skills;
- that helped them once again to perform well in their jobs;
- that led to another promotion or a more challenging assignment;
- and that repeated itself, again and again.

This success syndrome propelled the GMs into new positions about every 2.7 years, and virtually all changes brought more responsibility. Most spent the early parts of their careers in a single function which was somehow directly involved with some core aspect of their businesses. A minority rose through two functions, none through three or more. Most were promoted into their first general management jobs between the ages of thirty-four and forty; only one took his first GM job earlier than this, and three others later. As such, with only a few exceptions, these men entered general management relatively early in their careers and, in a sense, specialized there. Within general management, most further specialized within a very limited range of GM jobs or GM job contexts. Specifically, most of the GMs had held only one of the seven types of GM jobs in their careers. None had held more than two types. In terms of product-market age, none had held a GM job in both a very young and a very old context. In terms of size, only a few had held GM jobs in both very small and very large contexts.

Finally, all but one of the GMs were also clearly upwardly mobile in a socioeconomic sense. That is, they had already achieved a position and income greater than that of their fathers.

Two-thirds of them had already achieved a position and income substantially higher than had their fathers. Some, like P. J. Sparksman, whose father was a mail carrier, were earning as much as ten times more than their fathers had.

Although this list of background characteristics applies to all of the GMs in this study, some of these items much more closely describe the cases of the better performers. The better performers more often had fathers who were managers of people; more often reported having a very close relationship with a parent; more often had two or more siblings; more often had a graduate degree; more often joined companies which seemed to "fit" them well; more often developed a "success syndrome";[10] and more often developed strong mentors who helped them make the process a continuing one (none of the good/fair performers had mentors at the top of their organizations).

Possible Reasons for the Background Similarities

Again, there is some evidence from other sources that suggests that the similarities in backgrounds found here are not idiosyncratic to this group of GMs. For example, although some might think that the finding regarding tenure with one company is not the norm among most GMs, all the evidence I can find supports the findings of this study. Studies by Fortune,[11] Kron/Ferry International,[12] the Conference Board,[13] Arthur Young,[14] and others,[15] all show that top-level general managers tend to have spent most of their careers with their current employers. Other evidence,[16] including a recent study of over 200 CEOs in England,[17] supports still other patterns. Nevertheless, one might again wonder whether there is any logical reason for this set of patterns.

To understand how the background similarities might fit into this emerging picture, it is useful to consider how the personal characteristics in Figure 3.1 may have developed. One such plausible developmental dynamic is summarized in Figure 3.4. This developmental pattern suggests that the reason these GMs shared a number of background characteristics is because those experiences were responsible for shaping the personal characteristics that they shared—characteristics that helped them to cope effectively with difficult GM demands.

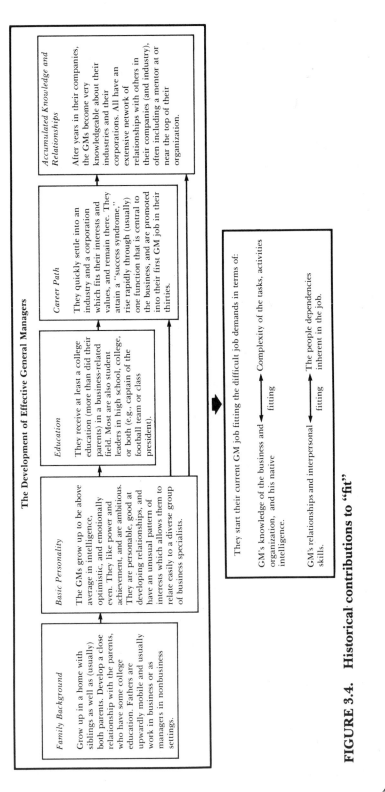

The Development of Effective General Managers

Family Background

Grow up in a home with siblings as well as (usually) both parents. Develop a close relationship with the parents, who have some college education. Fathers are upwardly mobile and usually work in business or as managers in nonbusiness settings.

Basic Personality

The GMs grow up to be above average in intelligence, optimistic, and emotionally even. They like power and achievement, and are ambitious. They are personable, good at developing relationships, and have an unusual pattern of interests which allows them to relate easily to a diverse group of business specialists.

Education

They receive at least a college education (more than did their parents) in a business-related field. Most are also student leaders in high school, college, or both (e.g., captain of the football team or class president).

Career Path

They quickly settle into an industry and a corporation which fits their interests and values, and remain there. They attain a "success syndrome," rise rapidly through (usually) one function that is central to the business, and are promoted into their first GM job in their thirties.

Accumulated Knowledge and Relationships

After years in their companies, the GMs become very knowledgeable about their industries and their corporations. All have an extensive network of relationships with others in their companies (and industry), often including a mentor at or near the top of their organization.

They start their current GM job fitting the difficult job demands in terms of:

GM's knowledge of the business and organization, and his native intelligence. ↔ fitting Complexity of the tasks, activities

GM's relationships and interpersonal skills. ↔ fitting The people dependencies inherent in the job.

FIGURE 3.4. Historical contributions to "fit"

Because the typical GM in the study had upwardly mobile, middle-class parents with whom he developed a close relationship, a father who worked in business or management and had some college education, and two or three brothers or sisters, from an early age the GM was exposed to the virtues of upward mobility, to education and business, as well as to superior, peer, and often subordinate relationships. In this environment, the GM logically could have developed considerable ambition, above average intelligence, an optimistic outlook, an emotionally even temperament, power and achievement motives, a personable style, skill at developing relationships, and a business set of interests.

In high school, the desire for power, the personable style, and related factors could have led the GM to become a student leader and would probably have made that experience a satisfying one. Ambition would have led him on to college and perhaps to graduate school. Interest in business might then have influenced the choice of a specialization (e.g., usually economics, business, or engineering).

After school the combination of ambition, a desire for power and achievement, good relationship skills, intelligence, optimism, and an even temperament would have helped him to do well early in his career, often leading to the development of helpful relationships with people in top management. These skills and hard work, those relationships, and possibly some luck could have led to a promotion into a general-management job early in his career.

Because he settled quickly into an industry and a corporation, and stayed there, by the time he was in his late forties the GM would have been very knowledgeable about that industry and that corporation. He probably also would have developed an extensive set of relationships within that industry and corporation for the same reason. These acquired characteristics, in combination with his earlier skills and personality, undoubtedly would have helped him to be effective in his work and contributed to his success and upward mobility.

Although he was very ambitious, the GM may not often have changed employers for a number of reasons. First, his detailed knowledge (of the business and the organization) and his extensive relationships probably were not transferable to another firm, and developing the needed knowledge and relationships quickly in a new firm would have been quite difficult. Hence, it would have been hard for him to have changed employers at a high level and still have been as successful and effective. Second, he may well not have been inclined to do so even if he could have successfully. In his early years, he may have learned something about the importance of commitment and loyalty that would lead him to want to stay with one corporate family. And, of course, he was doing well and was generally happy with his current company.

Of course, it is not possible to "prove" this last point about interfirm mobility any more than one can prove the other parts of the scenario suggested in Figure 3.4, but this developmental dynamic is certainly very plausible. It is consistent with findings from developmental psychology[18] and does offer one logical set of reasons for the similarities we have found in background characteristics of the general managers. And it has at least one very important implication—it suggests that the set of characteristics one needs to be effective in GM jobs requires a long time to develop; they do not emerge overnight. Events during an entire lifetime are important.

Differences in Personal and Background Characteristics

Paul Jackson and Michael Richardson were GMs with substantial responsibilities, both earned over $150,000 a year, and both had been very successful in their careers. They shared most of the characteristics shown in Figures 3.1 and 3.3. Nevertheless, they were very different in many ways.

Jackson's father was a farmer; Richardson's was a manufacturing executive. Jackson grew up in a Protestant household in the Midwest; Richardson's family was Catholic and lived in the East. Jackson was the second of three children; Richardson was the fourth of six. Jackson reports being very close to and very much influenced by both his parents; Richardson was somewhat less close to his parents. Jackson went to public schools and a state college where he received a BS in engineering; Richardson attended a private high school, and received undergraduate and graduate (MBA) degrees from two Ivy League schools. After school, Jackson spent some time in the navy. Richardson did not serve in the armed forces. During their early careers, Jackson worked in manufacturing and engineering; Richardson worked in finance.

Although I found both men to be interesting and likeable individuals, they struck me as quite different in a number of ways. Jackson was considerably warmer and more outgoing. Richardson, by his own admission, was somewhat shy. Jackson was considerably less analytical (and I would guess would score less on traditional intelligence tests); Richardson was "quick" and "bright." Jackson was more conservative; one could see this in his choice of clothes and office decor, and in his political views. Richardson was much more liberal and flamboyant. Jackson liked golf and woodcarving. Richardson preferred photography and ocean fishing.

As was the case with similarities, many of these and other differences among the GMs fit into reasonably clear patterns. Some are associated with age (or when they grew up), others relate to differences in the jobs they held. Still others are associated with the particular processes and circumstances when the jobs were filled.

Age-related Differences

Some of the individual differences among the GMs seem to relate strongly to when they were born and raised. More specifically, the seven older (mean age = 53) and the eight younger (mean age = 41) GMs were different in the following ways. The younger GMs came from homes with better-educated parents, with more professional or top-management fathers, and with more diverse religious backgrounds. They were more often the first-born children and were generally better educated. They were less likely to have served in the armed forces, more likely to have divorced their first wives, less likely to play golf, more likely to have working wives, and more likely to believe strongly that corporate and family life should be separated.

To a large degree these differences between the younger and the older GMs reflect broad social and economic changes that have occurred over the past thirty years. For example, the mean educational level of the population has been going up for generations now; hence it is not surprising that the younger GMs have somewhat better-educated parents and that they themselves are somewhat better educated than the older GMs. Nor is it surprising that the younger GMs tend to have served less often in the armed forces, to have married and divorced more often, to be a part of a dual career family, or to play tennis rather than golf, since these are trends that affected all people who grew up after World War II (the younger GMs were seven at the end of the war; the older GMs were nineteen).

Yet despite the fact that the differences between the younger and older GMs are not surprising if one considers the social and economic trends, the sheer number of age-related differences is nevertheless striking. This is so especially if one considers how rarely corporations acknowledge significant differences between younger and older executives.

Job-related Reasons for Individual Differences

In addition to age-related differences, it is possible to see a number of relationships between their personal differences and differences in their jobs. More specifically, different sets of job demands seem to be associated with different types of people (see Figure 3.5).

The patterns suggested in Figure 3.5 are an extension of the basic pattern identified in Figure 3.2, where we saw that the GMs tended to share certain characteristics that could probably be of great help in dealing with the key job demands identified and discussed in Chapter 2. It appears that as those demands vary somewhat, so do the individual characteristics.

For example, in the jobs where the responsibilities were more demanding and the decision making more difficult, I found GMs with a stronger set of those characteristics that all the GMs had to some degree to help them deal with the responsibilities inherent in the job: intelligence, analytical and intuitive skills, optimism, achievement orientation, knowledge of the business, and knowledge of the organization. Likewise, in jobs where the relationships were more demanding and accomplishing things more difficult, I found GMs with a stronger set of those characteristics which seem particularly useful in this regard: a personable style, skill at developing relationships, a liking of power, an emotionally even temperament, an ability to relate to a diverse group of business specialists, and extensive relationships in their organization and industry.

To some degree, these very general patterns can be seen in all

The GM Jobs

Responsibilities and Relationships

- Is responsible for a large, complex, and very diverse set of interdependent activities.

- Is dependent on superiors, a large and very diverse set of subordinates, and still others outside the chain of command.

Emergent Demands

- Figuring out what to do (making decisions) in an environment characterized by uncertainty, great diversity, and an enormous quantity of potentially relevant information.

- Getting things done through a large and diverse set of people (including bosses, subordinates and others) despite having little control over most of them.

Overall: An extremely demanding job, but one that provides status and income.

- In general, the personal characteristics tend to fit the key job demands

- The more demanding the decision-making issues, the stronger these personal characteristics tend to be.

- The more demanding the implementation issues, the stronger these characteristics tend to be.

- The larger the overall demands, the greater the ambition tends to be.

The GMs Personal Characteristics

Accumulated Information and Relationships

- Very knowledgeable about both their businesses and their organizations.

- All have extensive relationships throughout their organizations (and industry).

Basic Personality

- Above average intelligence, good analytical and intuitive skills, optimistic, and achievement oriented.

- Personable, like power, good at developing relationships, emotionally even, and have an unusual ability to relate to diverse groups of business specialists.

- Very ambitious.

FIGURE 3.5. Differences in GM characteristics that appear to be related to differences in the GM job

fifteen of the situations in this study. For example, Chuck Gaines had a job with unusually heavy relationship demands, primarily because of the large size of the organization and the type of job involved (product/market). In this relationally tough job I found a large and athletic-looking man who projected a strong presence. He was very skilled interpersonally and able to control his emotions almost completely. He seemed very comfortable exercising power, even more so than most of the other GMs. He also had strong connections in his corporation: his CEO was a mentor to him, and he had solid relationships with many others.

In the case of Bob Anderson, there were a different set of key job demands and a different type of person. Here the job had stronger than usual responsibility-oriented demands, basically because the business was in trouble and losing money when Bob took over. But because of the type of job involved (autonomous division GM) and the small number of people involved (and all in one location), the relationship demands were not unusually large. In this setting I found a GM who was more intellectual and analytical than most of the others in the study; he was also more of an optimist (less cynical than Gaines, for example). Because he had worked in his industry all of his professional life, he knew the business even better than most of the other GMs. But in terms of interpersonal styles, if Gaines could be likened to a lion, Anderson was a teddy bear.

The same general pattern helps explain, at least to some degree, the cases of Jackson and Richardson. Jackson had a product/market GM job for a diverse set of moderately mature businesses which employed many people. Relationally, it was an extremely difficult job. Recall that Jackson was quite skilled interpersonally, had been in the business all his life, and knew thousands of relevant people. Richardson, on the other hand, had helped start a business. In 1978, he was in a CEO's job in a small and relatively young context; his company was still charting its courses in new waters. Recall that Richardson was better educated than average and was considered rather intelligent. Even the basic values and philosophies of the two men fit their contexts. The more conservative and traditional Jackson worked in a midwestern, older, conservative company and industry. The more liberal and flamboyant Richardson worked in an eastern, younger, more liberal organization.

The patterns shown in Figure 3.5 *help* explain differences

among the GMs; they help one to see why a Jackson is found here and a Richardson there. But they do not explain all the differences, because the GMs did not always fit their jobs perfectly. Indeed, in most cases there was at least some degree of misfit. A closer examination of those cases suggests at least three common reasons for the degree of job-person misfit.

Main Factors Creating Misfits

One common reason why the GMs often had some characteristics which did not fit their job demands seems to be that those demands had changed in important ways while they were in the job. In these cases, an initially good fit eroded over time as businesses grew, or became more mature, or became more diverse. That is, the job demands changed but the GMs' abilities and inclinations did not change as much or in the same directions.

Another common reason for mismatches was that those who selected GMs sometimes did not think in terms of "fit." Although most modern personnel systems are built around this concept, only recently have some companies begun to consider that different kinds of GM jobs might require different kinds of people.[19] To some degree this is because business management researchers and theorists have rarely applied the concept of "fit" systematically to top-level management jobs.[20]

The most common reason for misfits was that, when the job had to be filled, an ideal person did not exist within the pool of candidates. That is, even though the decision makers tried to find an individual with characteristics that suited a specific GM position, they could not. Faced with no ideal candidate, the firms usually appear to have responded in one of two ways. Either they would take a less than perfect match from the executive pool, or they would look outside the pool, select a young star in their organization, and give him a big promotion (into the job that was somewhat over his head). Some firms made it a habit to move young stars rapidly and repeatedly into job after job that didn't yet fit them. Moving them this fast usually meant it was very difficult for them to acquire the skills, knowledge, and relationships needed to handle their increasingly larger responsibilities. As a result, they were all too often trying to "get up to speed" in a job, which usually meant longer work hours, less time for family and nonwork activities, and more stress.[21] When this condition continued for too long, the people involved began to show signs of "burnout."

In very small firms, it is not too difficult to see why one might have difficulty finding someone from the candidate pool to fit a GM job, simply because the pool itself will be very small. But in a large firm, which should have a large candidate pool, it is much more difficult to see why there should be a "shortage of needed management talent." Perhaps the most reasonable explanation for this exists in our finding of the long and complicated process by which successful general managers develop the characteristics they need to perform well in a GM job. Unless firms try carefully to manage that process, there is no reason why the candidate pool in even a large organization should have many people with the right characteristics in it. And none of the organizations in this study worked very hard or systematically at managing that developmental process.

Summary and Discussion

Most people, including the GMs themselves, think of a "specialist" as a person who concentrates his or her work in some functional area (accounting, finance, engineering, and the like). The GMs thought of themselves not as specialists but as generalists in the broadest sense of the word. As such, many of them felt they could handle a general management job in other companies, in other industries, or even in government. Many managers and academics apparently think along similar lines; they believe that a good "professional" manager can manage anything.[22] Few people have made an argument consistent with our findings here.[23]

Furthermore, an examination of trends shows no evidence that GMs are going to be any less specialized in the future. That is not to say that the type of people in GM jobs are not changing—quite the contrary. As we saw earlier in this chapter, the younger and older GMs were different in a number of ways that seems to reflect basic social and economic changes over the past thirty years. Nevertheless, there does not seem to be any difference in interfirm or interindustry mobility between the younger and older GMs. Both groups had spent about 90 percent of their career time in one industry and 80 percent of their careers in one company. Nor are there many differences in any of the other items listed in Figures 3.1 and 3.3.

Although we certainly cannot conclude that a person can only be effective in one narrow type of GM setting, this does suggest that even within the limited domain of GM jobs most GMs cannot be effective everywhere. Differences are important; fit is necessary. Specialization, which has a long history, seems to be the norm.

These findings have an interesting implication for the traditional "born" or "made" controversy. They suggest that neither proposition, as normally articulated, is really accurate. The "born" argument usually asserts that the circumstances into which one is born determine later success. The "made" proposition states that events independent of birth circumstances determine success. Typically, "made" proponents argue that some single factor such as education, or a mentor in one's company, or a lucky break early in one's career determine success. In the case of successful general managers, the reality appears more complex than either argument. Successful GMs appear to have been both "born" to circumstances favorable to the acquisition of GM characteristics and then "made" through a long series of events over a period of decades. No single event, by itself, seems to have been the key. The total series of circumstances appear to have been necessary to produce the characteristics needed to cope with difficult GM job demands.

4

General Managers in Action: Part I—Similarities in Behavior

GENERAL-MANAGEMENT JOBS do not come with a blueprint of what the incumbent should do. Job descriptions, when they do exist, tend to be vague and to emphasize end results rather than necessary actions. Management literature does not provide much guidance either. As Ken Andrews once noted:

> Theories of general management have consisted of exhortations to plan, organize, integrate, and measure, for example, with little being communicated on how to perform these grand functions in concrete situations.[1]

Yet despite this lack of structure and direction, and despite differences in the businesses and industries involved, the GMs in this study behaved in some remarkably similar ways. There were many similar patterns in their basic approaches to the GM job and even in their use of time on a daily basis.

In this age of "management science," these common behaviors often look incredibly "unprofessional." That is, the way the GMs in this study mobilized their special assets to cope with difficult job demands looks less systematic, more informal, less reflective, more reactive, less well organized, and more frivolous than a student of strategic planning systems, time management, MIS, or organizational design might expect. Nevertheless, this behavior worked; by all available measures these executives were doing either a good, very good, or excellent job (see Appendix E).

In this chapter we will first describe the common ways in which these managers approached their jobs; then we will look at similarities in daily behavior.[2] Throughout we will explore why they behaved this way and why this seems to be associated with good performance.

The major theme in this chapter can be summarized as such. Behavior which can at first look inefficient or unmanagerial or simply inexplicable takes on an entirely different appearance when considered in light of our discussion of the real nature of GM job demands and of the type of people found in these jobs. Indeed, the behavior reported here follows directly and logically from that previous discussion.

The Approach

All the GMs in this study approached their jobs in roughly the same way. During the initial period in the job they focused simultaneously on developing agendas for their businesses and on developing the networks of resources needed to accomplish those agendas. When the agendas and networks were largely in place, they then devoted much of their attention to making sure that the networks actually did implement their agendas.

Agenda Setting

The GMs always started their jobs with some knowledge of the businesses involved and some sense of what needed to be done with these businesses, but rarely did they have a very clear agenda in mind. Rarely did they have many goals, strategies, and plans for their businesses and organizations. But during the first six months to a year, they usually focused much of their activity on developing just such an agenda; later they continued to update their agendas, but in a less time-consuming process.

The agendas that these managers developed tended to be made up of a set of loosely connected goals and plans which addressed their long-, medium-, and short-run responsibilities. As such, the agendas typically addressed a broad range of financial, product/market, and organizational issues. They also included both vague and very specific items. Figure 4.1 summarizes the contents of a typical agenda.

For example, Bob Anderson's agenda included items directed at completing the installation of a new computer system, restructuring a part of his organization, further developing the team of people that reported to him, coping with an upcoming NLRB election, meeting quarterly sales and earnings targets for his corporation, finalizing a yearly set of objectives with each of his direct reports, and expanding his business via acquisition. These and other items were guided by some broad revenue, income, and market-share objectives which he thought could be achieved within five years.

Although all but one of the organizations involved had a formal planning process which produced written plans, the GMs' agendas always included goals, priorities, strategies, and plans that were not in the written documents. This is not to say that the formal plans and the GMs' agendas were incompatible; generally, they were rather consistent. They were just different in at least three important ways. First, the formal plans tended to be written mostly in terms of detailed financial numbers; the GMs' agendas tended to be less detailed in financial objectives and more detailed in strategies and plans for the business or the organization. Second, formal plans usually focused entirely on the short and moderate run (three months to five years); GM agendas tended to focus a bit more on a broader time frame, including the immediate future (1–30 days) and the longer run (5–20 years). Finally, formal plans tended to be more explicit, rigorous, and logical, especially regarding how various financial items fit together; GM agendas often contained lists of goals or plans that were not as explicitly connected.

For example, one of the GMs had a written five-year plan for his business that needed a sheaf of paper about one inch thick. Over 90 percent of the written plan was made up of financial statements of various kinds: sales forecasts by product line, expense and capital budgets by department and subdepartment, and so on. As a result of lengthy interviews with this manager, I learned that his own agenda was different in at least the following important ways. First, he did not expect two of the product lines to be as successful as the written plan projected, although he had trouble explaining exactly why he believed this to be so. Second,

Key Issues

Time Frame	Financial	Business (Product/Market)	Organizational (People)
Long-run (5-20 years)	Usually contains only a vague notion of revenues or ROI desired in ten or twenty years.	Usually only a vague notion of what kind of business (products and markets) the GM wants to develop.	Usually vague. Sometimes includes notion about the "type" of company the GM wants and the caliber of management that will be needed.
Medium-run (1-5 years)	Typically includes a fairly specific set of goals for sales and income and ROI for the next five years.	Typically includes some goals and plans for growing the business, such as: • see that three new products are introduced before 1981 • explore acquisition possibilities in the area of . . .	Usually includes a short list of items such as: • by 1982 will need a major reorganization • before 1981, I need a replacement for Corey
Short-run (0-12 months)	Typically includes a very detailed list of financial objectives for the quarter and the year in all financial areas; sales, expenses, income, ROI, etc.	Usually includes a set of general objectives and plans aimed at such things as: • the market share for various products • the inventory levels of various lines	Typically includes a list of items such as: • find a replacement for Smith soon • get Jones to commit himself to a more aggressive set of five-year objectives

FIGURE 4.1. The contents of a typical GM's agenda

he expected one of the lines to be more successful than written projections. Third, he expected that within three years one product line might have to be abandoned (one of those which he expected not to achieve the written plan). If that should be the case, he expected that within two years he would acquire one of three known alternative replacements. Fourth, he expected he would lose one of his subordinates to a corporate post within twenty-four months and planned on finding a way to transfer another subordinate (whose performance he felt was inadequate) out of his division within twelve months; reference to these changes was not in the written plan. Fifth, he expected that within five years the division would require a significant reorganization in order to accommodate its growth and changes in its business; the reorganization activity was not mentioned in the written plan.

The process by which these agendas were developed began immediately after the GMs started their jobs, if not before. The GMs used their knowledge of the businesses and organizations involved, along with new information received each day, to quickly develop a rough agenda. Typically this contained a very loosely connected and incomplete set of objectives along with a few specific strategies and plans. Then, over time, as more and more information was gathered, the agendas incrementally (one step at a time) became more complete and more tightly connected.

Four of the GMs in this study—Chuck Gaines, B. J. Sparksman, John Cohen, and John Thompson—were new in their jobs when I visited them. In gathering information for agenda-setting purposes, these GMs relied largely on discussions with other people rather than on reading books, magazines, or reports. These people tended to be individuals with whom they had relationships, not necessarily people in the "appropriate" job or function (such as a person in the planning function). They obtained information in this way by continuously asking questions, day after day, not just during "planning meetings." And they did so by using their current knowledge of the business and organization (and management in general) to help them direct their questioning, not by asking broad and general questions. That is, each found ways within the flow of his work days to ask a few critical questions and to receive in return some information that would be useful for agenda-setting purposes.

For example, I watched one of the GMs use the contacts he

had developed as the head of an industry association to learn about the strengths and weaknesses of two competing equipment suppliers whose products he was considering buying. I saw others learn about the operating and interpersonal problems in one of their units by talking to people they knew who were two or three levels below them in the hierarchy. I watched another learn about important corporate priorities by talking to a friend and peer in another part of the company. In some of these cases, I could not even understand the questions (until they were later explained to me) because I did not have a detailed enough understanding of the specific products, customers, competitors, financial arrangements, people, technology, management systems, or history involved. But the person whom the GM asked always did. Although the answers did not always provide new or important information, over a period of months the total volume of new and useful information appears to have been reasonably high.

With this information, the GMs appear to have made agenda-setting decisions both consciously/analytically and unconsciously/intuitively. Indeed, the GMs' agendas appear to have been created and modified in a process which was largely internal to their minds (both conscious and unconscious) and which went on continuously.

In one typical case, while a GM in this study took part in a series of meetings on inventory management problems, he decided that he would have to reduce his goals for December inventory levels and that he would seriously have to consider, sometime during the first part of the year, replacing one of his managers. But he verbalized neither decision, and anyone watching the process would have been completely unaware of what was happening in his mind. Even the manager himself was largely unaware of the second decision; it was developed intuitively. When I talked to him about the meeting at the end of the day, the manager almost did not mention the replacement issue; only at the very end of our conversation did he say, "I guess I also decided there and then that I was going to have to replace Phil." When I pressed him as to why, he had difficulty responding.

In selecting specific programs or projects or activities to include in their agendas, the GMs seem to have looked for possibilities which could accomplish multiple goals at once, which were consistent with all other goals and plans, and which they had the power to implement. Projects and programs that seemed "important" and "logical" but did not meet these criteria tended to be discarded or at least resisted.

For example, while I was visiting Tom Long, a subordinate tried on two occasions to start a discussion about a pet project of his. On both occasions, the GM simply shifted the conversation to another matter. Tom later told me that in his judgement the project would not contribute significantly to any of his major goals, even though it sounded good on the surface. Furthermore, as he put it, "It would require an enormous amount of time and energy to implement it."

A typical example of a project chosen because it could simultaneously accomplish multiple objectives was Chuck Gaines' "road show." Soon after he started his job, Gaines decided to create a major "show" for his dealer organization and to travel with the show to eight large U.S. cities. This project, which was expensive but required little internal cooperation since it was largely created and implemented by subcontractors, accomplished the following for Gaines:

1. It gave the dealer organization a moral boost which it needed since their industry had recently experienced a number of problems.
2. It allowed Gaines to meet or reestablish relationships with dealers under favorable conditions.
3. It gave Gaines the opportunity to signal to the dealers the new directions he would be taking his organization.
4. It allowed him the opportunity to try to influence a few key dealers directly to change certain historical practices.
5. It gave his staff the chance to show dealers a few new products.

To a large degree, the key to finding projects like this one seems to be timing. A project which was eminently successful could often have accomplished few objectives and been very difficult to implement if selected earlier or later than it was. The GMs all seemed to recognize that few programs or activities are always inherently good. The key is to find the right item at the right time.

This entire agenda-setting process is summarized in Figure 4.2. Although these patterns are not widely recognized in today's conventional wisdom on management, there is evidence from other studies that GMs and other top managers other than those in this study do use such a process.[3]

Almost all of the GMs in this study behaved as shown in Figure 4.2, but the better performers did so to a greater degree and with more skill. For example, the "excellent" performers developed agendas based on more explicit business strategies that addressed

FIGURE 4.2.   Agenda setting

I.   THE CONTENT: the GMs created agendas that

- were characterized by loosely connected goals and plans, based on (implicit or explicit) business strategies

- addressed long-, medium- and short-run time responsibilities

- included a broad range of business issues (e.g., products, finance, marketing, personnel, etc.)

- included both vague and specific goals and plans, as well as ones for others and themselves

- were largely unwritten

- were related to but different from formal written plans

II.   THE PROCESS: the GMs created agendas by

- aggressively gathering information (mostly from people with whom they already had relationships)

- asking these people questions on a continuous basis (not just in formal planning meetings)

- using their current knowledge of the business and organization (and management in general) to help guide the questioning

- making choices through conscious/analysis and through unconscious/intuitive processes (especially the latter)

- looking for specific programs, projects, and activities that could help accomplish multiple objectives at once, and that they had the power to implement

- doing the above in a continuous and incremental manner that is most time consuming during the first six to twelve months in a GM job

---

longer time frames and that included a wider range of business issues. They did so by seeking information from others (including "bad news") more aggressively, by asking questions more skillfully, and by more successfully finding programs and projects that could help accomplish multiple objectives at once.

Network Building

In addition to agenda setting, the GMs all allocated significant time and effort early in their jobs to developing a network of cooperative relationships to and among those people they felt were actually needed to accomplish their emerging agendas. Even after the first six months, this activity still took up considerable time, but generally, it was most intense during the first months in a job. After that, attention tended to shift toward using the networks both to implement and to help update the agendas.

This network-building activity, as I observed it and as it was described to me, was aimed at much more than direct subordinates. The GMs developed cooperative relationships to and among peers, outsiders, their bosses' bosses, and their subordinates' subordinates. Indeed, they developed relationships with (and sometimes among) any and all people upon whom they felt dependent because of their jobs. That is, just as they created an agenda that was different from, although generally consistent with, formal plans, they also created a network that was different from, but generally consistent with, the formal organization structure.

The networks developed by the GMs often included hundreds or thousands of individuals. The typical GM network was so large that it defied my efforts to draw one in any detail; a summary representation is shown in Figure 4.3

In these large networks, the nature of the relationships obviously varied significantly in intensity and in terms of basis; some relationships were much stronger than others, some much more personal than others, and so on. Indeed, to some degree, every relationship in a network was different because it had a unique history, it was between unique people, and so forth.

For example, B. J. Sparksman's network can be described briefly as such. He had a good working relationship with his four bosses and a close mentor-protégé relationship with one of

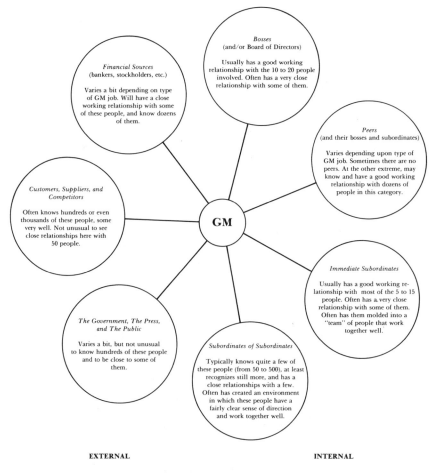

FIGURE 4.3.   A typical GM network

them. He had cordial-to-good relations with his peers, some of whom were friends and all of whom were aware of his track record and his mentorlike relationship to one of the three people who ran his organization. He also had a good working relationship with many of the subordinates of his peers (hundreds of people), based mostly on his reputation. B.J. had a close and strong working relationship with all but one of his main direct reports because they respected him, because he was the boss, and because he had promoted some of them into their current positions; those men also had strong cooperative relationships among themselves (they thought of themselves as a team). At least one of his direct reports looked to B.J. as a mentor and adviser, and was particularly close to him. B.J. also knew the vast majority of his subordinates' subordinates, if only by name, and had good relationships with them based on his reputation, the fact that he was the boss, and the fact that he tried to treat them fairly and with respect. Outside the firm, B.J. maintained fairly strong relationships with dozens of top people in firms that were important clients for his organization. By and large, these people seemed to find B.J. competent and charming in his own way. He also had relationships with dozens of other important people in his local community, which he had acquired through his participation on civic projects, on charity boards, and similar activities. These people tended to see B.J. as a "fine" person and as a good resource (for raising money, for example).

In choosing with whom to develop cooperative relations, the GMs seem to have selected people they felt could help them with their emerging agenda. The more dependent on an individual or group of people they felt, the stronger the relationship they tended to develop with them.

Frank Firono was typical in this regard. When I was first with him, he had been at his job for seven months. During the three days I was there, he spent more time developing and maintaining relationships with a subordinate's subordinate and an outside supplier than he did with two of his own direct subordinates. In each case, this reflected a judgement on his part regarding how important each of these people really were to his job and his emerging agenda. As he told me:

> Ralph [one of his subordinates] isn't going to be with us much longer. . . . George [another subordinate] doesn't have much to contribute, unfortunately. . . . Phil [the subordinate's subordinate] has a great potential for assuming more responsibilities and doing an excellent job. . . . I have known David [the outsider] for years, and he's been very helpful at times. I expect he will continue to be in the future.

The GMs developed these networks of cooperative relationships using a wide variety of face-to-face methods. They tried to make others feel legitimately obliged to them by doing favors or by stressing their formal relationships. They acted in ways to encourage others to identify with them. They carefully nurtured their professional reputations in the eyes of others. They even maneuvered to make others feel that they were particularly dependent on the GMs for resources, or career advancement, or other support.

For example, during my visits with the GMs I watched some, like Paul Jackson, build relationships (including with me) by using disarming candor. Others used their offices to help, by decorating them to be warm and inviting or powerful and overwhelming. Some used their charisma very effectively. Almost all skillfully found ways to do small favors for others—which cost the GMs little but was very much appreciated by the recipients.

Although all the GMs used these methods, virtually none talked about them. In some cases, I'm sure they simply were not aware of how they built and maintained relationships; in other cases, I suspect that they had learned that it was better not to talk about such things.

In addition to developing relationships with existing personnel, the GMs often developed their networks by moving, hiring, and firing subordinates. Generally, they did so in order to strengthen their ability to get things done. Dan Donahue was typical in this regard. Shortly after he took over his job he replaced two key subordinates, one because he felt the person could not do the job, and the other because the person was very disappointed for not getting the GM job himself. He also replaced a few other lower-level managers in sales "to strengthen the department."

In a similar way, they also changed suppliers or bankers, lobbied to get different people into peer positions, and even restructured their boards in order to improve relationships to needed resources.

Furthermore, the GMs sometimes shaped their networks by trying to create certain types of relationships *among* the people in various parts of the network. That is, they tried to create the appropriate "environment" (the appropriate norms and values) they felt was necessary in order to implement their agendas. Typically this was an environment in which people were willing to work hard on the GMs' agenda and cooperate for the greater good. Although the GMs sometimes tried to create such an environment among peers or bosses or outsiders, most often they did so with respect to their subordinates.

For shaping the environment in which subordinates worked, the GMs employed a number of different methods. For example, Gerald Allen and Bob Anderson both instituted MBO type systems. A few, such as Richard Poullin, changed the formal reporting systems to highlight the measures they felt were the most important and created measurement systems where they didn't exist before. Some actually modified the formal organizational structure. A few (like Richard Papolis) consciously tried to manage the "culture" of the organization. In a similar vein, some of the GMs influenced the environment under them by becoming a visible symbol of what they wanted others to be or to do. That is, they used both formal management tools such as planary processes, organizational structure, and control systems, as well as more informal methods to create the environment they wanted.

Poullin and Papolis, whose performances were rated excellent (see Appendix E), were particularly aggressive and successful in this regard. For example, Richard Poullin created an environment in his organization which others characterized with words like "teamwork," "clear signals," "good delegation," "meritocracy," "very analytical," "goal oriented," "not a personality cult," and "no politics." He did so by being a role model, by rewarding and encouraging people who behaved as he wanted them to and by getting rid of people who did not.

The overall process employed by the GMs in the study to create their networks is summarized in Figure 4.4. Although there is not a great deal of supporting evidence elsewhere, some which is consistent with these findings does exist.[4]

As was the case with agenda setting, almost all of the GMs behaved as shown in Figure 4.4 but the better performers did so more aggressively and with more skill. The "excellent" performers, for example, created networks with many talented people in them and with stronger ties to and among their subordinates. They did so by using a wider variety of methods with great skill. The "good/fair" performers tended to rely on fewer of the network building methods, did so less aggressively, and in the process tended to create weaker networks.

Execution: Getting Networks to Implement Agendas

After they had largely developed their networks and agendas, the GMs in this study tended to shift their attention toward using their networks to implement their agendas. They did so by using

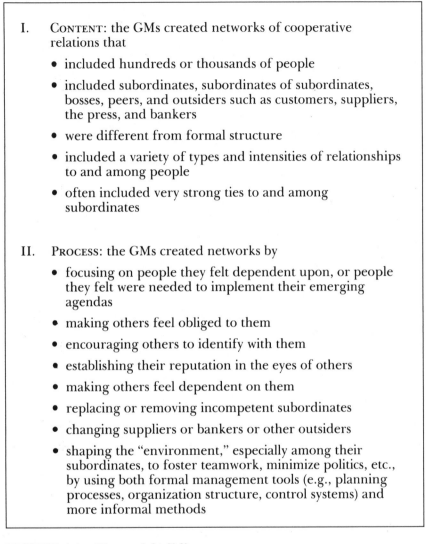

I.   CONTENT: the GMs created networks of cooperative
     relations that

   • included hundreds or thousands of people

   • included subordinates, subordinates of subordinates,
     bosses, peers, and outsiders such as customers, suppliers,
     the press, and bankers

   • were different from formal structure

   • included a variety of types and intensities of relationships
     to and among people

   • often included very strong ties to and among
     subordinates

II. PROCESS: the GMs created networks by

   • focusing on people they felt dependent upon, or people
     they felt were needed to implement their emerging
     agendas

   • making others feel obliged to them

   • encouraging others to identify with them

   • establishing their reputation in the eyes of others

   • making others feel dependent on them

   • replacing or removing incompetent subordinates

   • changing suppliers or bankers or other outsiders

   • shaping the "environment," especially among their
     subordinates, to foster teamwork, minimize politics, etc.,
     by using both formal management tools (e.g., planning
     processes, organization structure, control systems) and
     more informal methods

FIGURE 4.4.   Network building

their networks along with their interpersonal skills, budgetary
resources, and information to influence people and events in a
variety of direct and indirect ways.

In implementing their agendas, the GMs tended to call on
virtually their entire network of relationships to help them; they
did not limit their assistance to direct subordinates and a boss.
When necessary, they used any and all of their relationships. Dur-

ing my time with the GMs, I saw some of them call on peers in their companies, corporate staff people, subordinates reporting three or four levels below them, bosses reporting two or three levels above them, suppliers or customers, and even competitors to help them get something done. There was no category of people that was never used. And in each case the basic pattern was the same:

- the GM was trying to get some action on items in his agenda that he felt would not be accomplished by the network without active intervention on his part;
- the people he approached could be of help, often uniquely so;
- the people he approached were a part of his network;
- the people and the approach selected were chosen with an eye toward achieving multiple objectives at once and doing so without inadvertently disturbing important relationships in the network.

The GMs in this study, and especially the better-performing ones, did not waste time and energy intervening where it wasn't really necessary; they gave people who were capable of doing a good job the authority to do just that. They actively involved themselves in execution only when they felt something on their agenda would not be accomplished without their aid. And they chose execution strategies with an eye on achieving multiple objectives in their agendas at a minimum cost to their networks. (Probably the single most common reason that the GMs rejected staff [or consulting] advice was because they felt it would cost more in terms of strained relationships in their networks than it was worth in light of their agendas.)

Having approached people, the GMs often influenced them simply by asking or suggesting that they do something, knowing that because of their relationship with the person he or she would comply. In some cases, depending on the issue involved and the nature of the relationship, they also used their knowledge and information to help persuade these people. Under other circumstances, they would sometimes use the resources available to them to negotiate a trade. And occasionally they would even resort to intimidation and coercion (Chuck Gaines, for example, got reluctant corporate staff to do what he wanted by speaking very forcefully, often running over their sentences, and never backing down). Most readers will have seen all of these direct-influence methods used.[5]

The GMs also often used their networks to achieve more indirect influence on people, including people who were not a part of that network. In some cases, the GMs would convince one individual (who was in their network) to get a second individual to take some needed action. More indirectly still, the GMs would sometimes approach a number of different people, requesting them to take actions which would then shape events to exert influence on an individual (or group of individuals) to do something.

Perhaps the most common instances of indirect influence involved staging an event of some sort. In a typical case, the GM would set up a meeting or meetings and influence others through the selection of participants, the choice of an agenda, and often by his own participation. For example, Bob Anderson held weekly one-on-one meetings with each of his subordinates; the agenda was always the same: (1) to go over what had and had not been accomplished that past week, and (2) to set priorities and goals for the next week. The very process of these meetings led subordinates to do what he wanted. In a similar way, Tom Long achieved a lot of influence by having regular meetings, by concluding the meetings with an explicit statement of what people promised to do, by sending out memos with those promises after the meetings, and by reviewing those memos at the start of each subsequent meeting. In general, a number of GMs aggressively used this type of "follow-up" to get things done.

Unlike the direct influence, the GMs achieved much of their more indirect influence by using symbolic methods. That is, they used meetings, architecture, language, stories about the organization, time, and space as symbols in order to communicate messages indirectly. Chuck Gaines' "road show" which was mentioned earlier is a good, if somewhat dramatic, example of this. To influence his dealer organization in certain important ways, Gaines created a day-long event which was then staged in eight major cities across the U.S. This event included a two- to three-hour Broadway-like show which featured professional actors, carefully conceived scripts, and elaborate sets. Everything about the production symbolized prosperity; the implicit message was: the future is bright, now is a good time to expand your operations. Of course, the very same message could have been delivered much more directly (and cheaply) via short letters and phone calls, but the latter would not have been nearly as effective.

The overall pattern of execution is summarized in Figure 4.5. All the GMs in this study behaved this way, but the better performers did so more than the others and with greater skill. The better performers tended to mobilize more people to get more things done and did so using a wider range of influence tactics. The "excellent" performers asked, encouraged, cajoled, praised, rewarded, demanded, manipulated, and generally motivated others with great skill in face-to-face situations. They also aggressively relied on indirect influence more than did the others. The "good" managers tended to rely on a more narrow range of influence techniques and applied them with less finesse.

Once again, this type of behavior has been recognized and discussed in some management literature,[6] but not in very much of it.

FIGURE 4.5.   Executing: Getting networks to implement agendas

---

I. CHOOSING WHAT TO ACT ON. The GMs

- selected items on agendas that were not being effectively attended to by networks

- selected people in the networks who could help get action on those items

- selected an approach to influencing others which accomplished multiple objectives at once, and

- selected an approach which minimally disturbed important relationships in the networks

II. INFLUENCING THOSE PEOPLE. The GMs did so

- directly, by approaching a network member who could help on some agenda items and using their relationships to influence the person by asking, demanding, cajoling, intimidating, etc.; and

- indirectly, by shaping an event or a set of events by directly influencing a number of people, and by using time and space, meetings, architecture, language, and stories as symbols

---

Underlying Reasons for the Basic Approach

The approach taken to their jobs by the GMs in the study follows directly from our discussion in the previous two chapters, especially from Chapter 2, where we saw that the general-management job presented the incumbent with two fundamental dilemmas:

- figuring out what to do despite uncertainty, great diversity, and an enormous quantity of potentially relevant information; and
- getting things done through a large and diverse set of people despite having little direct control over most of them.

Because these dilemmas are inherent in the job, one simply cannot go about the work of "planning, organizing, staffing, directing, and controlling" in a simple, straightforward, and formal way that focuses on formal plans, the structure of subordinate roles, and the like (see Figure 4.6). One probably must adopt an approach somewhat like that of GMs in the study or fail.

Forces Behind the Agenda-setting Process

Because of the decision-making demands inherent in the job, some map or plan or agenda is absolutely necessary for reasons well recognized by traditional management thought; but because of the complexity and the uncertainty that is involved, formal planning can be very difficult to do well. Unlike the case in more routine and bounded jobs, it is often impossible to make reasonable projections upon which to build complete plans. It is also difficult to know what information is needed and how to get it. And there is just so much potentially relevant information.

Furthermore, formal systematic planning can exacerbate the implementation dilemma. As Terry Franklin told me:

> A problem with formal planning is that it gets people to think about hypothetical choices and the consequences of those choices to the organization, and more importantly, to themselves. This can lead to conflict and political activity which can be very damaging to the company. Written plans can also produce a problem because they take on the nature of "writing in stone." They rigidify people's expectations. People make plans based on those expectations. Then if

	Dilemmas Inherent in the Job	
Implications for Traditional Management Functions	Figuring out what to do despite great uncertainties, great diversity, and an enormous quantity of potentially relevant information.	Getting things done through a large and diverse group of people despite having little direct control over most of them.
Planning	Planning is very difficult to do well in such a context. It requires lots of time and attention, not just a series of meetings once a year. It requires a good information system to sort out the noise and focus on essential data.	Planning must be done in a way that does not exacerbate the already very difficult human environment. One must therefore be very careful regarding what is put on paper or said to others.
Staffing and Organizing	Some type of sound plan or map is essential, because without it there is no rational basis for "staffing and organizing."	The resources one needs to get the job done include many people besides direct subordinates. Hence, some form of "staffing and organizing" activity must be aimed at many others, and that will have to rely mainly on methods other than formal staffing and organizing procedures.
Directing and Controlling	Some type of sound plan or map is essential, because without it, it is impossible to know where to direct one's attention among the infinite possibilities. Without it, one cannot know what to direct or control.	A fairly strong set of cooperative relationships to those resources upon which one is dependent is essential, or one simply will not be able to "direct" and "control."

FIGURE 4.6. Behavioral implications, given the nature of GM jobs, for the traditional management functions of planning, staffing, organizing, directing, and controlling

the world changes, and you have to change the plan, you run into great resistance. Don't misunderstand me now. I'm not suggesting that formal planning is bad or unnecessary. Quite the contrary; it's absolutely necessary. But it's not enough by itself. And you have got to be careful regarding what to include in the planning.

In other words, the very nature of the GM job requires something similar to the agenda-setting process found here. Furthermore, according to our discussion in the last chapter, and to cognitive psychology,[7] the GMs seemed well suited to conduct such a process. They had the knowledge and relationships to launch the process, and the intellectual and interpersonal skills to execute it successfully.

Forces Behind the Network-building Process

The GM job places the incumbent in a position of dependence on a lot of people over whom he has little direct control. Under those circumstances, developing, maintaining, and shaping an informal network of relationships is probably essential. Without such a network, getting things done (implementing the agenda) may well be impossible. One is not in a powerful enough position; the network gives one power.

Furthermore, because of the complex nature of the responsibilities inherent in GM jobs, such a network may also be essential for agenda-setting purposes. In a sense, the networks these GMs created were incredible information-processing systems. They kept the GMs in touch with their responsibilities in a way that no formal or machine-based information-processing system could ever hope to do. These networks were capable of filtering masses of information and of passing on to the GMs only that which was potentially important for agenda-setting purposes.

In terms of the process, because of the scope and difficulty of the network building task, the approach the GMs used is probably the only feasible one. If there were fewer people involved, and if one had more time, a GM could probably build an adequate network without having to resort to some of the less straightforward, more coercive, more manipulative, and more time-consuming methods. But such is not the reality of GM jobs today.

Although some people would have neither the skill nor the inclination to do all this, the discussion in Chapter 3 suggests that these GMs all did. They had the interpersonal skills and the power motivation, both of which would seem to be necessary. In other words, as was the case with agenda setting, the job seems to demand such a network-building process and the GMs all had the skill and inclination to do so.

Forces Behind the Execution Process

In light of the way GMs approach agenda setting and network building, and in light of the nature of GM job demands, the execution process follows in a rather straightforward way. Having developed networks that are capable of implementing their agendas, it is not surprising that the GMs would make sure that they did so. And when something on the agenda was not being attended to, or not being dealt with efficiently, it seems logical that the GMs would have intervened to try to change the situation. Given the nature of the job, "intervening" means influencing people. In light of the size and complexity of the typical job context, it also seems reasonable that a GM would be forced to rely on the power of his relationships and his interpersonal skill to achieve that influence, and that he would need to use a wide variety of both direct and indirect methods. Given the sheer amount of influence made necessary by large job demands, it seems logical that one would look for efficiencies, such as by selecting an approach which accomplishes multiple objectives at once. Finally, given the composition of the network and the time required to build and maintain it, it seems reasonable that an effective GM would be very sensitive not to destroy important relations in it inadvertently while trying to execute.

In less uncertain and interdependent contexts, one can imagine a managerial approach to execution which is quite different from that used by the GMs in this study. Such an approach would be more straightforward, less subtle, and would use fewer methods. But the contexts in which these GMs operated were simply not amenable to such an approach.

Manifestations of This Approach in Daily Behavior

The way in which this approach manifested itself in day-to-day behavior can be clearly seen in the nearly 4,000 pages of notes I took while observing the GMs. Over a period of approximately two years, I spent more than 500 hours actually watching the daily activity of the GMs in this study. I watched them come to work, run meetings, travel, read their mail, write memos, and talk to dozens and dozens of people. Buried in these notes are twelve visible patterns in how they used their time each day.

The Twelve Visible Patterns in How They Used Their Time

Almost all the GMs in this study behaved in a number of similar ways which were relatively easy to observe. The twelve patterns include the following:

1. *They spent most of their time with others.* The average GM spent only 24 percent of his working time alone and this was usually at home, on an airplane, or while commuting. Only two of the GMs (Franklin and Poullin) spent less than 70 percent of their time with others. Most of the GMs spent much of their work days talking and listening to others; a few spent up to 90 percent of their work time this way.

2. *The people they spent time with included many in addition to their direct subordinates and bosses.* It was not unusual to find a GM talking to a subordinate's subordinate, a boss's boss, a customer or supplier, or an outsider with no formal relationship to his company. The GMs regularly went around the formal chain of command, and they also regularly saw people who often appeared to be relatively unimportant outsiders.

3. *The breadth of topics they covered in discussions with these people was extremely wide.* The GMs did not limit their focus to planning, business strategy, staffing, and other "top-management" concerns. At various times, they discussed virtually anything and everything even remotely associated with their businesses and organizations.

4. *In these conversations, the GMs typically asked a lot of questions.* Occasionally, in a half-hour conversation, some of the GMs (like Dan Donahue) would ask literally hundreds of questions.

5. *In these conversations, the GMs rarely seemed to make "big" decisions.* My students "make" more big decisions in their case discussions in one day than most of the GMs could be seen making in a month.

6. *These discussions typically contained a considerable amount of joking, kidding, and nonwork-related issues.* The humor was often about others in the organization or industry. Other nonwork discussions were usually about people's families, hobbies, or recent nonwork activities (golf scores, etc.).

7. *In not a small number of these encounters, the substantive issue involved was relatively unimportant to the business or organization.* That is, the GMs regularly engaged in activities that even they regarded as a waste of time.

8. *In these encounters, the GMs rarely gave "orders" in a traditional sense.* That is, they seldom "told" people what to do.

9. *Nevertheless, the GMs frequently engaged in attempts to influence others.* But instead of "telling" people what to do, they asked, requested, cajoled, persuaded, and intimidated.

10. *In allocating their time with others, the GMs often behaved in a "reactive" mode.* The major part of the typical GM's day was not planned in advance. Even the GMs who had a heavy schedule of preplanned meetings (such as Chuck Gaines, Tom Long, and Paul Jackson) often ended up spending a lot of time discussing topics not on the official agenda.

11. *Most of their time with others was spent in short and disjointed conversations.* It was rare to see a discussion of a single question or issue last more than ten minutes. And it was not at all unusual to see five minute interactions that covered ten unrelated topics.

12. *They worked long hours.* The average person worked just under sixty hours per week; only three of the fifteen GMs worked fewer than fifty-five hours per week (Allen, Thompson, and Papolis). Although some of their work was done at home, while commuting to work, or while traveling, most of the time was just spent at their place of work. (The average GM traveled only four and a half days per month. Only two of the fifteen [Gaines and Martin] traveled more than six days per month.)

A Specific Example

The following is an example of how these patterns manifested themselves in a day in the life of one of the GMs in this study. The GM in this case is Michael Richardson:

7:35 AM   He arrives at work (he does not have a long commute), unpacks his briefcase, gets some coffee, and begins a "to-do" list for the day.

7:40   Jerry Bradshaw, a subordinate, arrives. Bradshaw's office is right next to Richardson's; he has two sets of duties, one of which is as an assistant to Richardson.

7:45   Bradshaw and Richardson have an informal conversation on a number of topics. Richardson shows Bradshaw some pictures he recently took at his summer home.

8:00   Bradshaw and Richardson talk about a schedule and priorities for the day. In the process, they touch on a dozen different subjects and issues relating to customers, other subordinates, and suppliers.

8:20   Frank Wilson, another subordinate, drops in. He asks a few questions about a personnel problem and then joins in the previous discussion. The discussion is straight-forward, rapid, and occasionally is punctuated with humor.

8:30   Fred Holly, Richardson's boss, stops in and joins in the conversation. He also asks about an appointment at 11:00 and brings up a few other topics.

8:40   Richardson leaves to get more coffee. Bradshaw, Holly and Wilson continue their conversation.

8:42   He's back. A subordinate of a subordinate stops in and says hello, the others leave.

8:43   Bradshaw drops off a report, gives Richardson instructions to go with it, and leaves.

8:45   His secretary arrives. They discuss her new apartment and arrangements for a meeting later in the morning.

8:49   He gets a phone call from a subordinate who is returning his call of the day before. They talk primarily about the subject of the report he just received.

8:55   He leaves his office and goes to a regular morning meeting that one of his subordinates runs. There are about thirty people there. Richardson reads during the meeting.

9:09   The meeting is over. Richardson grabs one of the people there and talks to him briefly.

9:15   He walks over to the office of one of his subordinates (corporate counsel). His boss is there, too. They discuss a phone call the lawyer just received. While standing, the three talk about possible responses to a problem. As before, the exchange is quick and occasionally includes some humor.

9:30   Richardson goes back to his office for a meeting with the vice chairman of another firm (a potential customer and supplier). One other person, a liaison with that firm and a subordinate's subordinate, also attends the meeting. The discussion is cordial and covers many topics from their products to foreign relations.

9:50   The visitor leaves. Richardson opens the adjoining door to Bradshaw's office and asks a question.

9:52   His secretary comes in with five items.

9:55   Bradshaw drops in with a question about a customer and then leaves.

9:58	Frank Wilson and one of his people arrive. He gives Richardson a memo and then the three begin to talk about the important legal problem. Wilson does not like a decision that Richardson has tentatively made and is arguing for him to reconsider. The discussion goes back and forth for twenty minutes until they agree on the next action and schedule it for 9:00 tomorrow.
10:35	They leave. Richardson looks over papers on his desk, then picks one up and calls his boss's secretary regarding the minutes of the last board meeting. He asks her to make a few corrections.
10:41	His secretary comes in with a card to sign for a friend who is sick. He writes a note to go with the card.
10:50	He gets a brief phone call, then goes back to the papers on his desk.
11:03	His boss stops in. Before they can start, he gets a brief call. After the call he tells his secretary that someone didn't get a letter he sent and to please send another.
11:05	Holly brings up a couple of issues, and then Bradshaw comes in. The three start talking about Jerry Phillips, who has become a difficult personnel problem. Bradshaw leads, telling the others about what he has done over the last few days regarding this issue. Richardson and Holly ask questions. After a while, Richardson begins to take notes. The exchange, as before, is rapid and straightforward. They try to define the problem and outline alternative next steps. Richardson is not sure what is best so he lets the discussion go on, roaming around and in and out of the topic again and again. Finally, they agree on a next step.
12:00	Richardson orders some lunch for himself and Bradshaw. Bradshaw comes in and generally goes over twelve items. Wilson stops by to say that he had already followed up on their earlier conversation.
12:10	A staff person stops by with some calculations Richardson has requested. He thanks her and has a brief pleasant conversation.
12:20	Lunch arrives. Richardson and Bradshaw go into the conference room to eat. Over lunch they pursue business and nonbusiness subjects; they laugh often at each other's humor. They end the lunch focusing on a major potential customer.

1:15   Back in his office, they continue the discussion of the customer. Bradshaw gets a pad and they discuss a presentation to the customer in detail. Then Bradshaw leaves.

1:40   Working at his desk, Richardson looks over a new marketing brochure.

1:50   Bradshaw comes in again and they go over another dozen details regarding the presentation to the potential customer.

1:55   Jerry Thomas comes in. He is a subordinate of Richardson and has scheduled some key performance appraisals this afternoon in Richardson's office with him present. They briefly talk about how they will handle each.

2:00   Fred Jacobs (a subordinate of Thomas's) comes in. Jerry runs the meeting; he goes over Fred's bonus for the year and the reason for it. Then the three of them talk about Fred's role in the upcoming year. They generally agree and Fred leaves.

2:30   John Kimble comes in. The same format is used again. Richardson asks a lot of questions and praises Kimble at times. The meeting ends on a friendly note with general agreement.

3:00   George Houston comes in. The basic format is repeated.

3:30   When George leaves, they talk briefly about how well they had accomplished what they wanted in the meetings. Then they talk briefly about some other of Jerry's subordinates.

3:45   Richardson gets a short phone call. His secretary and Bradshaw come in with a list of brief requests.

3:50   He receives a call from Jerry Phillips. Richardson gets his notes from the 11 to 12 meeting on Phillips. They go back and forth on the phone talking about lost business, unhappy subordinates, who did what to whom, what should be done now. It is a long, circular, and sometimes emotional conversation. Near the end Jerry is agreeing with Richardson and thanking him.

4:55   Bradshaw, Wilson, and Holly all step in. Each is following up on different issues that were discussed earlier in the day. Richardson briefly tells them of his conversation with Phillips. Bradshaw and Holly leave.

5:10	Richardson and Wilson have a light conversation on three or four items.
5:20	Jerry Thomas stops in; he describes a new personnel problem and the three of them discuss it. More and more humor finds its way into the conversation. They agree on an action to take.
5:30	Richardson begins to pack up his briefcase. Five people stop by briefly, one or two at a time.
5:45 PM	He leaves the office.

Job-related Reasons for the Similarities

The patterns in daily behavior that Richardson's day illustrates are basically consistent with other studies of managerial behavior,[8] especially those of high level managers.[9] Nevertheless, as Henry Mintzberg has previously pointed out,[10] at least on the surface, this behavior seems hard to reconcile with traditional notions of what top managers do (or should do). It is hard to fit the behavior into categories like "planning," "organizing," "controlling," "directing," "staffing," and the like. And even if one tries, two conclusions seem to surface: (1) the "planning" and "organizing" that these men do does not seem very systematically done; it seems rather hit or miss, rather sloppy; and (2) a lot of behavior ends up being classified as "none of the above." The implication is that these are things that top managers should not be doing. Nevertheless, this is precisely how planning, organizing, and other functions manifest themselves in the daily behavior of effective executives.

To understand why we find this behavior and to identify still other but more subtle similarities, we need first to reflect back on the previous presentation in this chapter and information related in earlier chapters.

Patterns Directly Related to Their Approach to the Job

Most of the visible patterns in daily behavior seem to be direct consequences of how GMs approach the GM job, and thus consequences of the nature of the job itself and the type of people involved. More specifically, some of these patterns seem to derive from the approach taken to agenda setting, others from network building, others from how they tend to use networks to implement agendas, and still others from the approach in general (see Figure 4.7).

The very first pattern (spending most of the time with others) seems to be a natural consequence of the GM's overall approach to the job and the central role the network of relationships plays. As we saw earlier in this chapter, the GMs develop a network of relationships with those upon whom the job makes them dependent and then use that network to help create, implement, and update an organizational agenda. As such, the whole approach to the job involves interacting with people; hence it should not be surprising to find that on a daily basis, as the Richardson example clearly shows, the GMs spend most of their time with others.

Likewise, because the network tends to include all those upon whom the GM is dependent, it is hardly surprising to find the GM spending time with many besides a boss and direct subordinates (pattern #2). And because the agenda tends to include items related to all the long-, medium-, and short-run responsibilities associated with the job, it is to be expected that the breadth of topics covered in daily conversations might also be very wide (pattern #3).

A few of the other patterns seem to be a direct consequence of the agenda-setting approach employed by the GMs. As we saw earlier, agenda setting involves gathering information on a continuous basis from network members, usually by asking questions. Pattern #4 (GMs ask a lot of questions) follows directly. With the information in hand, we saw that the GMs created largely unwritten agendas. Hence, major agenda-setting decisions are often invisible; they occur in the GM's mind (pattern #5).

We also saw that network building involved the utilization of a wide range of interpersonal tactics. Since humor and nonwork discussions can be used as effective tools for building relationships and maintaining them under stressful conditions, we should not be surprised to find these tools used often (and we do—pattern #6). Since maintaining relationships requires that one deal with issues that other people feel are important (regardless of their centrality to the business), it is also not surprising to find the GMs spending time on substantive issues that seem unimportant to us and them (pattern #7).

The GMs' Approach to the Job

- *Overall,* it centers around the development of a network of relationships with those the job makes the GMs dependent upon, and the use of that network to create, implement, and update an agenda.

- That *network* tends to include most or all those the GMs are dependent upon, including bosses, subordinates, peers, and outsiders.

- That *agenda* tends to include items dealing with all the areas in which the GMs are responsible.

- *Agenda setting* involves gathering information on a continuous basis, usually by questioning network members on the wide range of topics relevant to the GMs' responsibilities. The GMs then create an unwritten agenda in an invisible process (decision making occurs in his mind).

- *Network building* involves the use of a wide range of tactics; the use of humor is one such widely used tactic. Network maintenance often involves taking time to work on issues that are not important to the business, but are to specific important individuals.

- In *using the network to implement the agenda,* the GMs use a wide variety of direct and indirect influence methods; giving "orders" in a traditional sense is only one of them.

Daily Behavior

1. They spend most of their time with others.

2. The others include many besides a boss and direct subordinates.

3. The breadth of topics covered in conversations with others is very wide.

4. In these conversations, the GMs ask a lot of questions . . .

5. yet they very rarely can be seen making big decisions.

6. The discussions typically contain a considerable amount of joking and non-work-related issues.

7. The substantive issues involved in these discussions are often relatively unimportant to the business or organization.

8. In these encounters, the GMs rarely give orders....

9. but they often try to influence others.

FIGURE 4.7. The relationship of some daily behavior to the GMs' approach to the job

87

We also saw that after the initial period on the job, the thrust of the GMs' approach was to use their networks to implement their agendas. They did so using a wide variety of direct and indirect influence methods. Ordering was only one of many methods. Under these circumstances, one could expect to find them rarely ordering others (pattern #8) but spending a lot of time trying to influence others (#9).

The Efficiency of Seemingly Inefficient Behavior

Of all the visible patterns in daily behavior, perhaps the most difficult to understand, or at least appreciate, are #10 (the GMs do not plan their days in advance in much detail; they react) and #11 (conversations are short and disjointed). On the surface at least, these patterns seem particularly unmanagerial; yet they are possibly the most important and efficient of all the daily patterns.

The GM job can be very demanding. GMs say they could spend over 100 hours per week on the job if they did not find ways to control their time; but somehow they manage to keep the 100+ hours down to an average of fifty-nine (pattern #12).

The agendas and networks the GMs develop seem to be central to their ability to contain their time demands. These devices allow the GMs to be somewhat opportunistic on a daily basis, to react to the flow of people and events around them in an efficient way, yet to do so knowing that they are still contributing more or less systematically to a longer run plan.

The following is a typical example of the effectiveness and efficiency of "reactive" behavior. In this case Jack Martin, on his way to a meeting, bumped into a staff member (who did not report to him) near the elevator. Using this opportunity, in a two minute conversation he: (a) asked two questions and received the information needed in return; (b) helped to reinforce their good relationship by sincerely complimenting the manager on something he had recently done; and (c) got the manager to agree to do something that Jack needed done. The agenda in Jack's mind guided him through this encounter. It allowed him to ask important questions and to make an important request for action. At the same time, his relationships with this member of his network allowed him to get the cooperation he needed to do all this so quickly. Had Jack tried to plan this encounter in advance he would have had to set up a meeting; setting up and conducting the meeting would have taken at least fifteen to thirty minutes, or 750 to 1500 percent more time than the chance encounter. And if he had not already had a good relationship with the person, the meeting might have taken even longer or not been effective at all.

In a similar way, the agendas and networks allowed all the GMs to engage in short and disjointed conversations that were often extremely efficient. The following very short set of discussions, taken from a day in John Thompson's life, are typical in this regard. These occurred at about 10:30 one morning in Thompson's office; with him were two of his subordinates, Phil Dodge and Jud Smith:

> THOMPSON: What about Potter?
> DODGE: He's OK.
> SMITH: Don't forget about Chicago.
> DODGE: Oh yeah. (Makes a note to himself.)
> THOMPSON: OK. Then what about next week?
> DODGE: We're set.
> THOMPSON: Good. By the way, how is Ted doing?
> SMITH: Better. He got back from the hospital on Tuesday. Phyllis says he looks good.
> THOMPSON: That's good to hear. I hope he doesn't have a relapse.
> DODGE: (leaving the room) I'll see you this afternoon.
> THOMPSON: OK. (to Smith) Are we all set for now?
> SMITH: Yeah. (He gets up and starts to leave).
> LAWRENCE: (stepping into the doorway from the hall, speaking to Thompson) Have you seen the April numbers yet?
> THOMPSON: No, have you?
> LAWRENCE: Yes, five minutes ago. They're good except for CD, which is off by 5 percent.
> THOMPSON: That's better than I expected.
> SMITH: I bet George is happy
> THOMPSON: (laughing) If he is, he won't be after I talk to him.
> WILSON: (his secretary, sticking head into doorway) Phil Larson is on the phone.
> THOMPSON: I'll take it. Will you ask George to stop by later? (others leave and Thompson picks up the phone) Phil, good morning, how are you. . . . Yeah. . . . is that right. . . . No, don't worry about it. . . . I think about $1,500,000. . . . Yeah. . . . OK. . . . Yeah, Sally enjoyed the other night, too, thanks again. . . . OK. . . . Bye.
> LAWRENCE: (stepping back into the office) What do you think about the Gerald proposal?

THOMPSON: I don't like it. It doesn't fit with what we have promised corporate or Hines.

LAWRENCE: Yeah, that's what I thought, too. What is Jerry going to do about it?

THOMPSON: I haven't talked to him yet. (turning to the phone and dialing) Let's see if he's in.

This set of conversations may look chaotic, but they are not very different from many daily conversations that most people have. They seem chaotic to us because we do not share the business or organizational knowledge these managers have, and because we do not know the GM's agenda. That is, we do not know who Potter, Ted, Phyllis, Phil Larson, Sally, Hines, or Jerry are. We do not know what exactly "Chicago" or "April numbers" or "CD" or the "Gerald proposal" refers to, nor do we know what role Potter or Hines plays in Thompson's agenda. If we did, the conversations would look very different.

But more important still, beyond being "not chaotic," these conversations are in fact amazingly efficient. In less than two minutes Thompson accomplished all of the following:

1. He learned that Mike Potter has agreed to help on a specific problem loan. That loan, if not resolved successfully, could have seriously hurt his plans to increase the division's business in a certain area.

2. He reminded one of his managers to call someone in Chicago in reference to that loan.

3. He also learned that the plans for next week, in reference to that loan, are all set; these included two internal meetings and a talk with the client.

4. He learned that Ted Jenkins was feeling better after an operation. Ted worked for Thompson and was a reasonably important part of his plans for the direction of the division over the next two years.

5. He learned that division income for April was on budget except in one area. That reduced pressures on him to focus on monthly income and to divert attention away from an effort to build revenues in one area.

6. He initiated a meeting with George Masolia to talk about the April figures. John had been considering various future alternatives for the CD product line, which he felt must get on budget to support his overall thrust for the division.

7. He provided some information (a favor) to Phil Larson, a

peer in another part of the bank. Phil had been very helpful to John in the past and was in a position to be very helpful in the future.

8. He initiated a call to Jerry Wilkins, one of his subordinates, to find out his reaction to a proposal from one of the other divisions that would have affected John's division. John was concerned that the proposal could interfere with five-year divisional-revenue goals.

In a general sense, John Thompson, Michael Richardson, and most of the other GMs in the study were, as Tom Peters recently put it, "adept at grasping and taking advantage of each item in the random succession of time and issue fragments that crowd (their) day(s)."[11] This seems to be particularly true for the better performers, and central to their ability to do so were their networks and agendas (see Figure 4.8). The agendas allowed the GMs to react in an opportunistic (and highly efficient) way to the flow of events around them, yet to know that they were doing so within some broader and more rational framework. The net-

FIGURE 4.8.   The efficiency of seemingly inefficient behavior

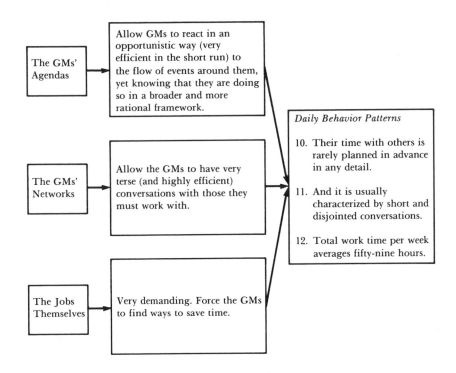

works allowed terse (and very efficient) conversations to happen; without them, such short yet meaningful conversations would have been impossible. Together, the agendas and networks allowed the GMs to achieve the efficiency they needed to cope with very demanding jobs through daily behavior patterns that on the surface look "unmanagerial."

Summary and Discussion

The overall pattern from this and previous chapters can be summarized as such. The GM job is a very demanding one, both intellectually and interpersonally. It seems to require and attract a certain type of person, a specialist of sorts, who has the personal characteristics that can deal with those demands. The nature of both those demands and those personal characteristics tends to lead to a certain approach to the job, and that in turn leads to certain commonalities in daily use of time. Examined individually, some of the specific findings (like the ones presented in this chapter) can seem odd, but when taken together, they seem to fit into a consistent and logical whole (see Figure 4.9).

If some commonly held beliefs about how top executives approach their work, or *should* approach their work, are often different from the patterns reported here, it is because these beliefs are also based on very different assumptions about the GM job and the GM, especially the former. For example, some common beliefs about how GMs should behave implicitly assume that the GM job is quite different from the jobs studied here, in that responsibilities and the activities associated with them are assumed to be: (a) smaller; (b) less diverse; and (c) more routine and predictable. In addition, relationships and the people associated with them are assumed to be: (a) smaller; (b) less diverse in character; and (c) a source of power (not of dependence). Under these much less complex circumstances we would expect to find effective GMs approaching their jobs differently. We would expect them to approach agenda setting in the more structured and analytical manner of a formal planning process. We would expect them to spend much less time on network building, and to rely on fewer, more accepted relationship-building methods (such as simply clarifying and stressing formal relationships, selecting good subordinates, etc.). Finally, in implementing and updating

The GM Job

Job Responsibilities and Relations

- Is responsible for a large, complex, and very diverse set of interdependent activities.

- Is dependent on superiors, a large and diverse set of subordinates and still others outside the chain of command.

Emergent Demands

- Figuring out what to do (making decisions) in an environment characterized by uncertainty, great diversity, and an enormous quantity of potentially relevant information.

- Getting things done through a large and diverse set of people (including bosses, subordinates and others) despite having little direct control over most of them.

The GMs

Accumulated Knowledge and Relationships

- Knowledgeable about their businesses and organizations.

- All have extensive relationships throughout the organization (and industry).

Basic Personality

- Above-average intelligence, broad interests, optimistic, achievement oriented, emotionally even.

- Personable, like power, good at developing relationships and have an unusual ability to relate to a diverse group of business specialists.

THEIR APPROACH TO THE JOB

Initially

- They use their current knowledge of the business and organization, their relationships with relevant others, and their intelligence and interpersonal skills to learn more about the job's complex demands and to create an agenda for the business and the organization. This is done in an ongoing (daily) informal process which involves a lot of questioning and produces a largely unwritten agenda of loosely connected goals and plans.

- Concurrently, they use those same personal assets to develop a network of cooperative relationships with those subordinates, bosses, and others upon whom the job makes them dependent. The greater the dependence, the more time and effort they devote to using a wide variety of methods for developing and maintaining the relationship.

Later

- They use their network of relationships to help them implement their agendas, using a wide variety of direct and indirect methods to do so. They also rely on their networks for information to update their agendas.

DAILY BEHAVIOR

1. They spend most of their time with others.
2. The others include many besides a boss and direct subordinates.
3. The breadth of topics covered in discussions with others is very wide. . . .
4. In these conversations, the GMs ask a lot of questions . . .
5. yet they very rarely can be seen making big decisions.
6. The discussions typically contain a considerable amount of joking and non-work-related issues.
7. The substantive issue involved in these discussions is often relatively unimportant to the business or organization.
8. In these encounters, the GMs rarely give orders . . .
9. but they often try to influence others.
10. Their time with others is rarely planned in advance in any detail . . .
11. and it is usually characterized by short and disjointed conversations.
12. Total work time per week averages fifty-nine hours.

FIGURE 4.9.   Factors influencing the behavior of GMs

these agendas, we would expect them to rely more on direct subordinates alone, to deal with them in a more straightforward manner, and to stress controlling and evaluating their efforts.

The reality, however, is that the responsibilities and activities associated with most management jobs, especially GM jobs, are becoming larger, more diverse, and less routine. Likewise, the relationships and people associated with the jobs are becoming larger in number, more diverse in character, and more a source of dependence (not of power). As such, in the future we might expect the basic approach described in this chapter to be even more pronounced.

5

General Managers in Action: Part II—Differences in Behavior

Tom Long and Richard Papolis both worked for the same large U.S. corporation and managers at corporate headquarters thought highly of both of them. By most standards, both were performing very well in their jobs and both had had very successful careers thus far; yet they seemed to operate so differently that some people at corporate (including my contact) wondered how they could both possibly be so effective.

I began to sense these differences even before meeting the two men. When I arrived at Long's office at 8:15 AM for our first encounter, scheduled for 8:30, he was busy with his 7:30 AM appointment. His secretary gave me coffee and an office to work in until 8:30 sharp. When I arrived at Papolis' office at 8:45 for our 9:00 AM first meeting, his secretary gave me coffee and cookies and had me wait in his office; he hadn't yet arrived. At 9:15 he did.

The two men worked in very different environments. Tom's office was modern, tastefully simple, and had clean working surfaces. Richard's office, at least compared to Tom's, was chaotic; there were no clean surfaces and the walls were covered with photographs, favorite sayings, and even pictures he had painted.

Tom's day was as well organized as his office. He spent most of his time in scheduled meetings. There was almost always a relatively clear purpose, and Tom was relentless in helping others achieve that purpose. His style had the rhythm and discipline of a first-rate military drill team: one, two, three, four, one, two, three, four.

Richard's day was quite different. He too had scheduled meetings, but they were far fewer in number; he spent much of his time in informal discussions with his subordinates, many of which they (not he) initiated. The pace was sometimes rapid, and sometimes quite relaxed. Voices were sometimes soft and sometimes very loud (Richard would occasionally yell at someone).

The content of their days was also different. Tom was more heavily involved in short-run issues, Richard in middle- and long-run questions. In addition to spending time dealing with subordinates, Tom spent considerable effort on lateral and upward relations, much more than Richard did.

Even the hours they worked varied considerably. Tom worked about sixty-five hours a week, usually starting at 7:00 AM and ending at 6:00 PM. Richard worked about forty hours a week and was proud of it.

Other managers in this study behaved in ways that were different from those of Long or Papolis. That is, although these GMs behaved in ways that were remarkably similar in some respects (as reported in the last chapter), they also sometimes approached their jobs and used their time each day in ways that were very different.

Later in this chapter we will examine the cases of Long and Papolis in some detail; but first we will explore in general the question of differences in behavior and of antecedents to these differences.

The Basic Patterns

The Range of Differences

There was considerable variation among the GMs in this study around the central tendencies described in the previous chapter. This variation is found in almost all aspects of behavior: in agenda setting, in network building, in execution, and in daily activities. This is particularly true in terms of four broad dimensions: (1) with whom [if anybody] they interacted; (2) on what issues; (3) for how long; (4) and how. In the extreme cases, the differences seem even greater than the similarities.

Regarding with whom they interacted, the following range of differences existed. Anderson's and Franklin's approach to their jobs led them to deal with only a few hundred people on a recurring basis, while Gaines and Long dealt with a few thousand. Probably three-quarters of the people Papolis dealt with on a typical day were subordinates (or subordinates of subordinates) while only about 5 percent of the people Martin saw were such. Most of the people with whom Richardson and Poullin interacted for agenda setting, network building, and executive purposes had graduate educations. Anderson and Gaines often interacted with people who had no college education at all.

In terms of the issues involved, the range of differences was again fairly large. Allen, Martin, and Long focused upwards of 90 percent of their attention on fairly short-run issues; Poullin and Papolis appear to have put less than 50 percent of their effort on such issues. Franklin and Gaines focused heavily on sales questions, while Donahue dealt mostly with new-product development issues. In their overall allocation of time some, like Papolis, spent considerable time on network building and maintenance (even though he had been on the job considerably longer than one year). Others, like Cohen, spent relatively little time on agenda setting (although he had been on the job only a few months).

In terms of the total time involved, although the average GM worked a fifty-nine hour week, there was again a wide range. Richardson and Sparksman worked seventy or more hours a week; Thompson and Papolis worked fifty or less.

Finally, in terms of how they used their time in interaction with people on various issues, there was a variety of styles. In agenda setting, some, like Donahue, relied very heavily on questioning others while others, like Franklin, did not. In network building some, like Papolis, used humor a great deal while others, like Long, went out of their way frequently to praise people for good work, In execution, some, like Gaines, were often forceful and could be very intimidating; others, like Martin, seldom behaved that way.

Antecedents

These kinds of differences in behavior appear to be the product of the same set of forces that created the similarities reported in Chapter 4. That is, differences in behavior were shaped initially by differences in job demands and differences in the personal characteristics of the GMs. Differences in job demands were in turn influenced by differences in job type, in the organizations involved, and the businesses involved (which were in turn shaped by the differences in the histories of those organizations and industries as discussed in Chapter 2). In a similar way, differences in personal characteristics were shaped by different personal histories (as discussed in Chapter 3). Later (six to twelve months) differences in behavior were shaped by those factors along with the differences in the agendas and networks that emerged. This is graphically summarized in Figure 5.1.

For example, in terms of job factors influencing behavior, the type of job and the size of the context were important as such. The people in product/market GM jobs (Martin, Jackson, and Gaines) set their agendas, developed their networks, and executed their agendas by interacting far more often with peers and outsiders than did those GMs in autonomous division-manager roles (Papolis, Firono, Cohen, Anderson, and Franklin). In doing so, they traveled nearly twice as much as did those in other types of GM jobs. On the other hand, GMs in operations GM jobs (Allen

FIGURE 5.1.   Dynamics responsible for differences in behavior

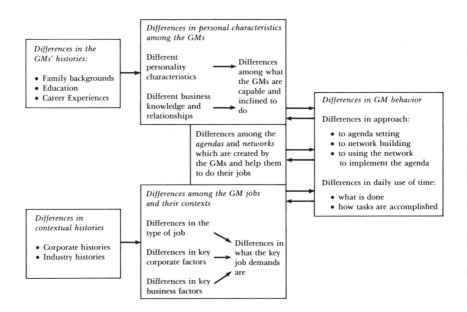

and Long) focused much more on agenda setting and execution of shorter-run issues than did most of the others. This was quite visible when I visited them. Regarding size, GMs in large settings tended to interact with many more people during agenda setting, network building, and execution than did GMs in small settings, and they tended to do so (out of necessity) in a more formal way; on a daily basis that typically meant more scheduled meetings.

In terms of personal factors, differences in business knowledge and relationships, for example, affected behavior in these ways. The GMs who started their jobs with more specific knowledge of their businesses and organizations and with more relevant relationships tended, during the first six months, to spend less time on agenda setting and network building and more time on execution. As a result, people promoted from within a division, like John Cohen, tended to work fewer hours during their first months than those promoted in from another part of the company (like Dan Donahue), and were faster in "making things happen."

After the GMs had been in their jobs for a while, differences in the agendas or networks which emerged influenced behavior in mostly straightforward ways. Differences in agendas created differences in what issues they dealt with; differences in networks created differences in whom they dealt with. And differences in how well the networks were capable of handling the agendas influenced differences in how much time and effort the GMs had to devote to execution (i.e., the bigger the gap, the more time and effort the GM tended to spend intervening in an attempt to make up the difference himself).

To appreciate the dynamics suggested in Figure 5.1 more fully, we must more closely examine a few specific cases. We will begin by looking at Tom Long; then we explore the case of Richard Papolis.

Tom Long

The Job and Its Context

In 1978, Tom Long was the Eastern Regional General Manager for International Computers. In this job, he was responsible for twenty sales-service offices spread over ten eastern states. Nearly 4,000 people worked in these offices.

International Computers was a $10-billion-a-year manufacturer of computers and computer-related equipment. The firm was founded in 1920 as a manufacturer of office machines; it remained relatively small until the 1950s when it first began to make computers. IC grew rapidly during the 1960s and captured a dominant position in its markets. By 1978, it was still growing at about 15 to 20 percent per year, but its market share had dropped from its peak in 1966, and it faced considerably more competition.

As one of four regional general managers, Tom reported to the head of branch operations at IC corporate (located in California). Reporting directly to Tom were three branch operations managers (each of whom supervised about seven branches), a technical services manager, a sales manager, a controller, and a personnel manager. In addition, one member of the company's legal staff was housed in the region's main offices, with a dotted-line relationship to the ERGM. No manufacturing or product-development personnel were in this part of the company.

Each of IC's four RGMs was held responsible for achieving over a dozen yearly objectives in areas related to sales, service, budget control, affirmative action, and net income. An elaborate measurement system regularly showed each region's (and each branch's) performance against objectives and ranked regions (and branches) in order of overall achievement.

The demands this situation placed on the ERGM were relatively severe, primarily because the context was fairly large, the products and markets were moderately young, and the firm's recent performance was only fair. But because of the type of GM job (operations), these demands were most concentrated in the areas of short-run decision making (operational control) and the management of subordinates.

Long-run demands (direction and policy-setting problems) were only mildly difficult, despite the growth rate of the company, the rate of new-product development, and the sophistication of the technology used, because of the type of job involved. Moderate-run issues (resource-allocation problems) were moderately severe, primarily because the company's growth rate put a strain on resources; but they were not highly demanding because the job lacked responsibilities in a number of areas, such as product development. Short-run demands (operational control problems), however, were severe owing to the type of job involved, the large volume of fairly complex activity going on (4000 people working with more than 100,000 customers spaced out over the entire East coast), the type of measurement system used by the corporation, and the heavy competition. In other words, a central challenge in this job involved keeping on top of a huge set of sales and service activities, making sure that those activities were "on plan," and taking corrective action quickly if they were not.

Because of the constantly changing nature of the business, appropriate goals for the region were a matter of judgement to be negotiated with corporate management. For this and similar reasons, demands associated with managing upward were moderately strong. The management of lateral relations was also moderately demanding due to the type of job involved (e.g., the region had to depend on manufacturing and product development done elsewhere). Finally, the management of subordinates was greatly demanding because of the large number of people reporting up to this position, the reasonably high education level (and expectations) of these people, the constant need both to retain and to attract more people (created by the growth rate), and other similar factors. As such, a second key challenge in this job involved motivating a large group of people in a moderately formal bureaucracy to meet or exceed sales, income, service, and other targets.

Tom

The person in this job during the winter of 1978–1979 was Tom Long. He was a good-looking and clean-cut young executive. He stands out in my mind today as an individual who was highly motivated, competitive, and ambitious; who was well-disciplined and in control; who was very skilled interpersonally and excellent "on his feet"; who had an eye for detail; and who was well organized.

Tom was born in 1942, the second of three children in a Protestant home. He was raised in Virginia and Florida primarily by his mother, with whom he developed a very close relationship. In high school he was the president of several clubs, was active in almost all sports, and won a number of awards associated with these extracurricular activities. Academically he performed in the top 40 percent of his class. Later, Tom received a BS in management from the University of Florida. While in college, he worked about twenty hours per week to help pay the bills. In his last two years, he made the dean's list.

After graduating from college Tom married Phyllis Bryan and began work for Fairchild Life Insurance Company, first as a trainee and then as a supervisor in the underwriting department. Two years later he accepted a sales job in another city with Phillips Manufacturing; he also started taking MBA classes at night. After one year at Phillips, Tom accepted an assistant sales representative position at International Computers. That job was followed by his rapid rise in the IC hierarchy.

In his twelve-year career at IC, Tom had held eleven different positions. His job titles were: assistant sales representative; sales representative; account representative; sales program manager; area sales manager; sales planning coordinator; special assistant to the head of branch operations; branch manager; branch operations manager (in a regional office); national service operations manager (at corporate); and eastern regional general manager. During this period Tom had won companywide awards for individual sales and for branch office sales. He had also moved geographically six times, divorced and remarried, and had five children. By 1978, he was thirty-six years old, and one of the youngest people at his level in the entire corporation.

Six people who knew him relatively well described Tom to me in the following ways. First, in terms of motivation, they said Tom was "very competitive," and "ambitious." Everyone seemed to know that someday Tom wanted to be the head of the firm. They also often commented on his high standards; as one put it, "Tom is more intolerant of incompetence than most managers I know."

In terms of temperament, they described him as "very disciplined," "intense," "strong willed," and "methodical." Some people even felt he was too intense for his own good. But one person noted that this intensity faded away off the job. He told me that Tom had "a terrific relationship with his wife and children and is much more relaxed with them than he is at work. He plans and takes vacations and enjoys them very much. He's the kind of guy you just don't call at home at night to talk about work."

With regard to cognitive style, they described him as "very precise," "thorough," "extremely well organized," "very bright," and "logical." One noted that he had "good business judgement." Some noted he had a tendency "to make up his mind quickly about things." A few even felt he drew conclusions "too quickly" at times.

Regarding interpersonal style, they described Tom as "charismatic," "super on his feet," "a good communicator," "very effective in groups," "able to motivate people very well," "very skilled in his use of recognition," and "good at picking people." They also agreed he was "terrific at making people feel accountable," and "big on follow-up." One person noted that his tendency was to be "aggressive upwards" and that he could also "relate well even to lower levels of management and staff and develop credibility and trust very quickly with people." Another noted that "he knew all the psychological tricks; he can be intimidating or charming or whatever he wants." Yet at the same time, he and others agreed that Tom's style was basically to be "straightforward with people." Said one, "He's very open; you always know where you stand." Said another, "He generally manages conflict by being very confrontive." Everyone agreed he was "fair and honest," and "extremely ethical." The only criticism people made of his interpersonal skills was that he did not "delegate enough at times."

In terms of relationships, they noted that Tom was "well respected by former subordinates," and had "good relationships with his bosses." One said he was "very visible to all his employees, not just those that report to him. He knows lots of people by name." Another told me that he respected Tom a great deal "because he's a winner." In terms of knowledge, they noted that Tom knew "all the management fundamentals, that is to say planning, organizing, etc." After twelve years at IC, he also knew the sales and service part of their business very well.

Tom's Approach to the Job

Tom's basic approach to his job as eastern regional general manager might be summarized as "driving the organization to maximum achievement" or "driving the organization to win." That is, he took the organization for which he was made responsible and aggressively directed and pushed and motivated it to "perform" at a very high level on dimensions dictated by corporate.

More specifically, in terms of agenda setting, Tom quickly created an agenda with a fairly short-run focus which was characterized by many detailed and ambitious goals. To a large degree, this agenda was imposed from above. The detail that he added was created by involving others in a fairly formal planning process and by relying on his own detailed understanding of the business to direct this process.

In terms of network building and maintenance, Tom used his existing relationships in the organization, his reputation, and his interpersonal skills to plug himself quickly into the large and complex network that already existed around the job. He did so by continuously being visible: making speeches to groups, visiting offices, and the like. In this way he developed a good professional reputation in which he was "respected by his subordinates" (according to most with whom I spoke) and had "solid relations" with most bosses and key peers. He also tried (in his words) to "create an environment [within the subordinates' part of his network] which provides the people in the region with the opportunity to achieve their objectives and also provides them with a job they enjoy."

Although Tom spent considerable time involved in agenda setting and network building, the bulk of his time, even after holding the job only six months, was spent on execution. He did so by skillfully using both carrots and sticks. He praised and pushed, recognized and intimidated, motivated and drove people to achieve. And above all, he followed up aggressively on a multitude of details. In doing so, he used his relationships, skills, and the formal systems with great effectiveness.

A great deal about Tom's style of execution can be seen in Figure 5.2; reprinted there is a typical memo that Tom sends out after his regular staff meetings.

Daily Behavior

I had a chance to see how this approach manifested itself in daily behavior during a three-day visit with Tom in September, 1978. On one of these days, we traveled to New York to visit a branch. On another, the morning was spent in a nearby hotel at a branch manager's meeting. On the third, Tom stayed at the regional headquarters. Tom dressed in conservative business suits on all three days.

INTERNAL MEMO

TO: Region Senior Staff   FROM: T. R. Long

SUBJECT: Senior Staff Meeting   DATE: September 14, 1977
                  Sept. 12 Follow-Up Actions

1. Jack Lynch is responsible for providing us with an integrated schedule of events for our Spring HRP update. This schedule should include all key dates including time frames for the development of our Panel Interview Process and questions. This schedule of events should be reviewed with us at our September 19th Staff Meeting.

2. It was generally agreed that the performance reporting system for branch profit and loss performance is unnecessary and confusing at this time. Mike Lewis agreed to follow-up with Gary O'Connell on delaying this program due to its inconsistency with current strategies.

3. Mike and I agreed to meet to establish a final schedule for our activity/ resource plan distribution. We will reserve one or two days for a thorough discussion of the total activity and resource plans. Although the resource plan may be discussed at a different time than the activity plan, the entire activity plan will be finalized in a one or two-day meeting.

4. We confirmed once again that each of you and all of our Branch Managers fully understand their responsibilities associated with their "opportunities to hire." With the emphasis we have placed on this responsibility over the past two months, all branches should achieve their affirmative action net addition responsibilities.

5. Our Branch Operations Managers agreed to meet with Carl Anderson and key members of his staff for a full Service review.

6. Mike Lewis agreed to provide us with an installation effectiveness report each Monday.

7. Paul Thompson is responsible for communicating the revised 1200 manpower plans to our branches reducing our plan to 95. This correspondence should be communicated by Friday, September 16th.

TL:sw

Tom

FIGURE 5.2.   A typical memo from Tom Long

On the day Tom stayed at the regional headquarters, he arrived at about 7:45 AM and left at 6:00 PM (he estimated that between the office, traveling, and at home, he worked an average of sixty-five hours a week). He spent most of the day in his office or in the adjacent conference room in scheduled meetings with people (he estimated that he spent about 80 percent of his time meeting with people). Tom's office was a corner office, measuring about 18 feet square; it was modern, tasteful, and uncluttered. Except for a few awards, plaques ("Excellence is a state of mind"), and pictures of his children, most surfaces were bare. The meetings on this day included:

- A one-and-three-quarter-hours scheduled meeting with one of the branch operations managers. This manager arrived with an agenda of six items, and Tom raised others during the meeting. These issues related to meeting certain sales objectives, dealing with some specific personnel problems, his learning from a training program that he had attended, performance appraisal, meetings scheduled for later in the month, and a question about a memo sent from corporate. The manager occasionally referred to a large black notebook he had brought with him.
- A two-hour scheduled meeting on planning and budgeting for 1979. Six people were included. The meeting focused on the logistics of the process over the next two months, on making sure that the goals set for their branches were appropriate, and on making sure that the process led to acceptance of the goals by the parties involved.
- A short meeting with a corporate staff person covering a dozen or more issues.

On the day of the branch manager's meeting, Tom spent much of the time listening to others' presentations. He also made a few speeches, gave out some awards, and orchestrated the overall event. His presence in front of the group was always well received.

On the day of his visit to the New York branch, Tom and the branch operations manager to whom the branch reported spent most of the flight to New York reviewing details about the branch. Both had thick notebooks to which they often referred. They talked about the branch's current performance, problems, and key personnel. After a short drive from the airport, they met the branch manager and nearly a hundred others at a hotel ballroom. The meeting, run by the branch manager, lasted approximately two hours. Although some information was given on new products and other subjects, the main purpose was to recognize good performance and to give out prizes. Tom's only active role in the meeting was to give out one prize.

After the meeting, Tom talked to a number of people, all of whom he knew by name. While the twenty-five managers in the branch sat down to eat lunch, he met in private with an employee who did not want to accept a transfer he was recently offered; half an hour later, both emerged smiling and announced he would accept the transfer.

After a quick lunch, Tom made a short speech to the managers and then asked for questions. For nearly two hours, he answered questions about a variety of subjects. He encouraged people to be open about their concerns and problems and dealt with the questions in what appeared to be a very straightforward and honest way. At the end, he received a warm round of applause.

Richard Papolis

Although Richard Papolis also worked for International Computers, his situation was quite different from Long's in many ways.

The Job and Its Context

In 1978 Richard was President of the Datatrack Division of International Computers. This division was created as an independent company in 1969 by Richard and four other people and was acquired by IC in 1976. Since its inception it had been growing rapidly; in 1978 the rate of growth was about 30 percent per year.

Datatrack had sales in 1978 of about $40 million. It employed over 650 people, most of whom were located at corporate headquarters near San Francisco. With nearly a 70 percent share of its market, Datatrack was the leading company in its part of the computer industry. The firm manufactured about forty related products, ranging in price from \$1,000 to \$70,000. These products, sold to thousands of customers all over the world, were all based on a single technology. Since the company's formation, the officers had believed that this technology would ultimately dominate their industry.

Datatrack was organized into eight groups that reported to Richard: marketing; engineering; research and development; finance; quality assurance; systems (software) development; manufacturing; and personnel. Four of these groups (marketing, R&D, engineering, and finance) were headed by men who had founded the company with Richard. The firm's organization had few formal policies, procedures, rules or regulations, but it had a strong "culture" that highly valued informality, boldness, innovation, caring about people, open communications, flexibility, and autonomy. Associated with this were numerous informal traditions which helped make the company, in the eyes of many employees, unique (see Figure 5.3).

Richard explained this:

> Our company is different from other companies that I have known, in a number of ways. For example, we are very sensitive to stupid policies. We try not to have a lot of rules. We have less structure than most companies and that which we do have is understood by people. We don't stand on formality; we don't try to scare people by wearing fancy suits. We make it clear that effort is not key, results are key. We talk a lot. Some of it is frivolous, but most of it is work related. We don't treat people in a moralistic way; we don't tell them what they should do. We don't have private parking places; I can walk as well as the next guy. Authority should be based on competence, not awe. We care for people because it's smart to care for people. Very few orders are given here and virtually no punishment. We don't like phonies; we throw them out after they've been here a very short period of time. We like the brutal truth. We don't bullshit each other. You'll find very little "Fix it, Richard is coming." We don't accentuate status and titles. We love to see a difficult challenge.

Datatrack was housed in two modern California-Spanish-style buildings near San Francisco. Most people in these buildings did not have private offices; what offices there were had glass windows in the doors and no locks. In the reception area and elsewhere were paintings by Richard. "Be bold" signs were on every wall and door. Most offices and desk areas also had many personal pictures, signs, or posters.

DATATRACK—ONE OF A KIND

Datatrack's five founders continue to shape our uniqueness, just as they have from the beginning. Their management style and philosophy, shared by fellow executive staff peers, combine to make Datatrack a very special place by observing practices that make good business sense, demonstrating an appreciation of people, and having a special enjoyment for things done in the spirit of fun.

OUR TRADITIONS

As our way of doing things is expressed in practices repeated through the years, they become traditions, uniquely Datatrack.

Flags Fly High

At our headquarters' main entrance we practice the colorful tradition of flying flags. We proudly display our state and national flags, and also feature another flag, appropriate to the day, which is chosen from our inventory of over forty selections.

The flags are used to welcome special visitors and to celebrate special days like St. Patrick's Day, for example. When International Computers personnel visit, you're likely to see the international symbol flag for the letters "IC" flying. And we're always glad to learn how pleased our foreign visitors feel to see the symbol of their homelands flying high in the California breeze.

Conference Rooms are Special

Our conference rooms are furnished with teak tables built by our president and his executive staff. Members of this group also devoted weekends to building a beautiful, 20-foot-long parquet-topped table and a functional refreshment center. Both pieces attractively fill Datatrack's largest meeting room—the Amber Room.

This room is not named because of an amber color, but as an honor to our founders. The word "amber" contains the first letter from the first names of each of Datatrack's five founders: Albert Thompson, Mike Dixon, Bob Allen, Eric Franklin, and Richard Papolis. Other conference rooms are creatively named Fantasia, the Sunshine Room, and the Gathering Room.

FIGURE 5.3.   Excerpts from "Inside Datatrack: An Employees' Handbook"

FIGURE 5.3. (*Continued*)

Special Events

As significant company milestones occur, coworkers enjoy celebrating together at fun-filled company parties featuring live music, refreshments, and lots of excitement. Or for example, Christmas might be highlighted by strolling carolers or the surprise gift of a Christmas ham for each employee. Datatrack's Halloween Costume Contest is another employee favorite.

When an employee reaches a fifth or tenth anniversary with Datatrack, we celebrate it! Our long-term employees are very special to Datatrack and to honor them each employee receives a special logo pin which is awarded by management.

To Our Way of Thinking

The company motto, "BE BOLD," appears everywhere. Even Datatrack's just-for-fun t-shirts spread the word in a rainbow of colors. This slogan conveys the philosophy that has made Datatrack the dynamic, successful company it is today.

One thing everyone likes about Datatrack is that management scorns the usual preferential reserved-parking spaces and "mahogany row" atmosphere. Instead, a comfortable friendliness prevails. Everyone is on a first-name basis.

We believe the longer you're acquainted with Datatrack, the more you'll agree we're a very special place to hang your hat.

Overall, this situation presented the CEO at Datatrack with a difficult set of job demands that were different in many ways from those Tom Long faced. This situation was smaller and younger, and it involved a different kind of GM job (autonomous divisional GM versus operations GM).

Long-run (direction and policy-setting) issues in Richard's case were much more demanding because of the type of job involved and the uncertainties created by the young product/market environment (by rapid growth, state-of-the-art technological development, and the like). Medium-run (resource-allocation) issues were also more demanding for basically the same reasons. Short-run (operational-control) demands were less severe, mostly because of the smaller size of the context.

Upward and lateral management demands were also less severe because of the type of job involved, because the division was once a completely autonomous entity, and because of the company's "good" performance in the eyes of IC management. But downward management was a reasonably big problem here, although for different reasons from those in Long's case. Here, managing subordinates meant managing potential conflict among a very diverse set of people (engineers and salesmen, old-timers and new hires) who had to work together despite the stresses of rapid growth. And it meant trying to maintain the culture despite the constant inflow of new employees.

Richard

The person I found in this job during the winter of 1978–1979 was an unusual, fascinating individual. He was flamboyant, had a wide range of talents, and was perhaps the most articulate person in the whole study on the topic of management. Richard had a philosophy of management about which he felt strongly and to which he had given much thought; Datatrack was a product of that philosophy.

Richard was born in Greece in 1927, the youngest of four children. He was raised there and developed a very close relationship with his father (a sea captain) and a close relationship with his mother. He attended high school in Greece and graduated in the upper third of his class. After a brief time in the Greek Navy, he came to the United States to attend UCLA, where he received both a bachelor's and a master's degree in physics.

After school, Richard worked for three years as an engineer at Johnson Research. He then married Katrina Nicholas and switched his employment to DLC Inc. At that firm he worked for five years as an assistant technical director. He then switched to Fairfield Lewin, where he worked as a technical director (for five years) and as a division manager (for eight years). In 1968, he became discouraged by Fairfield's unwillingness to exploit some opportunities he and his director of research had identified; so in 1969, he and four of his managers at Fairfield quit to form their own company (which they called Datatrack, Inc.). Richard became president, Albert Thompson the VP for engineering, Mike Dixon the VP for R&D, Bob Allen the VP for marketing, and Eric Franklin the VP for finance.

Datatrack manufactured its first small computer in 1970. That and subsequent machines were received very well by the market, so Datatrack grew very rapidly. In 1976, Papolis and his partners sold the company to International Computers, who then treated it as an autonomous division.

When I met Richard in 1978, he was still President of the Datatrack Division of International Computers. All of the original partners were still with the firm. Richard was then married to his second wife and had two teen-age children from his first marriage.

Those who knew Richard well described him as follows. In terms of motivation, most agreed he was a "driven man," who had "high standards," and enjoyed the "spotlight" of success. In terms of temperament, most said he was "optimistic," "emotional," "anxious," "impatient," and "strong willed."

Cognitively, one person noted that he had a great ability to identify patterns in complex situations. "For example, he'll say, 'You know, six months ago, you did such and such and that's happening again now, and it happened once last year, so maybe there's a pattern here.' " Another noted that he was very good "at spotting people problems, and he is usually right."

Interpersonally, most agreed he had a "superior ability to sense feelings, to know what offends people, what motivates people," etc. Some felt he was an "amateur psychiatrist." One person noted that he was "very personable. You get to know him as a person. You get to know his family. It all leads you to trust him, to feel you can trust him."

All agreed he was a very talented person. One told me that he thought Richard was the most talented guy he'd ever met. "He builds instruments, he sings, he cooks, he sails, he can do almost anything." Another noted that "few people can keep up with him, including his new young wife. He's a fabulous chef. Watching him cook, you can get a sense of his great timing." I certainly found him to be thoughtful, witty, and extremely quotable. A typical example: "The only way you can succeed in a business is to satisfy a need at a profit. If you satisfy a need at no profit, that's philanthropy. If you satisfy no need at a profit, then you're a crook."

Richard's Approach to the Job

Richard's basic approach to his general-management job was in some ways quite different from Tom Long's. Basically, he focused on maintaining the organization he had created and on keeping it on the right track; and he did so in a very informal, personal way.

Richard's agenda, which was largely developed by the early 1970s, took a long view of things. It did not include a great deal of detail or, for that matter, many specific goals. Instead, it contained general notions about what the company could become in five, ten, or twenty years; and it included a general strategy for how that would happen. For example, during one of my visits with Richard, he reported the following to me:

> We want and expect to become a very large and successful company in a relatively short period of time. We think this is an attainable objective for these reasons: First, the market for our products has been and will continue to grow at a rapid rate for years to come. No one disputes this projection—financial analysts, technical people, etc. Second, ultimately, the technology that will dominate this market will be the one that is the most cost-effective—that can do the job at the lowest cost. We believe that logically this means [the kind of technology they were using. He went on at this point to elaborate on this logic]. Third, we are the leading firm in the industry using this technology. No one is ahead of us in developing this technology. Therefore, if we can stay alive, and continue to keep our technological lead, we will ultimately achieve our goal. We will become very large and very profitable. Finally, we think we are well positioned to both stay alive and keep our technological lead because of the type of organization we have created.

Richard's network of relationships had been created by him over a long period of time. It was relatively small (compared to Long's, for example) and was mostly below him in the organization. Richard spent a lot of his time maintaining his network; that is, he spent considerable time both maintaining his organization and maintaining his strong ties to that organization. He did so, to a large degree, by focusing his attention on keeping people working together harmoniously, helping to get new people on board and up to speed, maintaining the culture, and the like. And he did all this in a way that was consistent with his philosophy and the company culture—informally, directly, and personally.

In maintaining his network, Richard focused a lot of his time on the founders. One person with whom I talked put it this way: "The primary reason that we have been so successful so far is because the top group of officers gets along so well. They talk things out until they are satisfied they've got the right thing to do. There's no political infighting. The group has excellent relationships; everybody pulls together to solve a problem. Richard is key here." Another manager observed that "under a different leadership I wonder if the conflicts among these people wouldn't be very damaging. Richard keeps this from becoming a problem."

Compared to many managers, including Long, Richard spent relatively little time at execution. As one manager told me: "The direction Richard gives the company is in its long-range strategy and in its philosophy. Within that, he gives you a lot of latitude."

Richard himself described his approach to network building and execution as follows:

> My job, as I see it, is to motivate people to do what I think fits in the overall plan. I order no one to do anything. I set up the conditions under which the required action takes place. The process is essentially an art. It involves finding out the grain of the situation and then going with it, not against it. It is much like sailing, which I enjoy very much. When I go sailing, I go with the wind. To achieve my goal, I have to study the situation, set the sails, and go with the wind and the water. It is much the same in management. I don't make big product or market decisions. I create the right conditions under which those decisions can be made. I think of myself as a gardener, as an arranger, as a creator of climate.
>
> People are very concerned with their images in the eyes of others. Therefore, in relating with people, the statements that are made are often meaningless. What is important is what they imply about a person's self-esteem. I spend a fair amount of my time trying to reduce contempt in the organization. It's absolutely deadly. Not conflict, but contempt. It's the ultimate in desecrating people's self-images. Contempt, for example, can easily develop in an organization like ours between the production and the marketing people. It is essential to keep a dialogue going between them. Many companies fail because they do not. Marketing, engineering, and production people often don't understand one another. It is not unlike the Jews and the Arabs. The key here is to build each group's esteem in the eyes of the other group. My role is to help make them interact with one another in a constructive way. The general manager's role is making sure that the dialogue happens.
>
> Overall, a manager's job is to affect behavior, not to leave people alone. This requires constant and frequent contact with people. I go around and see people every day. I'm usually not that busy. For example, we have orientation classes downstairs for new employees,

and I take part. That way I get to see all the new people. I also deal with crises and hold people's hands. Nobody ever falls in love with a manager, so I always oscillate between the role of boss and playmate. I'm also not afraid of firing people, although that rarely happens. Many people have thanked me for terminating them, pushing them into a verdict that is best for them. I mean, who wants to perform poorly?

Daily Behavior

This approach manifested itself in daily behavior that was considerably different from Tom Long's. During my visits with Richard, he usually dressed informally; he never wore a suit and tie. He generally arrived at work between 8:30 and 9:00 AM and left at 5:00 or 5:30 PM. He never took a briefcase full of work when he left in the evening. He sometimes took leisurely luncheons (two hours) away from the office building. Overall, he worked about forty hours a week. When I asked him about his work hours, Richard said, "I get the feeling that most executives feel guilty about how much money they make, so they work long hours to make them feel better. It's silly. Effort doesn't count. Results count."

Everyone from the receptionist to the vice president called Richard by his first name. When he walked around the Datatrack buildings he would usually talk to and kid around with a large number of people.

On a typical day Richard spent little time alone in his office (perhaps 10 percent of the day). Instead, he spent his time talking to people, usually in both large and small unscheduled meetings. During the time I was with him, these included:

- three discussions with his vice president of manufacturing, which sometimes included other manufacturing managers. (Shipping and personnel problems in manufacturing were the biggest issues at Datatrack at the time.) Richard initiated two of these discussions and worked with the managers to clarify what the problems were and how they should be addressed;
- the regular Wednesday 4:00 meeting of the officer group, which lasted for about three hours. For much of that meeting, Richard refereed an obvious fight between his marketing and manufacturing vice presidents;

- two discussions with the vice president of marketing, who was concerned about the manufacturing problem. Richard spent much of the time here trying to calm the man down and to get him to see things from manufacturing's point of view;
- two discussions with the vice president of finance. One involved a routine financial briefing, the other was initiated by the vice president of finance who wanted to tell Richard about his view of the "manufacturing problem";
- a meeting of about ten people on the major new product Datatrack was developing. Richard spent most of the meeting listening. He asked a few questions and left early;
- a meeting of about twelve people on a new product they were just starting to develop. Richard listened, asked questions, and expressed enthusiasm over most of the ideas presented;
- a discussion initiated by the vice president of personnel about a personnel problem;
- a meeting with the vice president of systems development and two of his people to look at a demonstration of a new product. Richard asked questions and praised them for a job well done;
- an unscheduled meeting initiated by Richard, attended by four of the officers and two others, to design a presentation for IC corporate.

These interactions were all characterized by lots of humor (initiated by everyone, but especially by Richard) as well as a good deal of directness, warmth, and informality.

While I was with him, Richard also had short telephone conversations with all his vice presidents and spoke on the phone to IC corporate about three times. On one of these mornings, he gave a speech to 350 high-school teachers in a nearby school district.

Long and Papolis: A Few Final Observations

Although the cases of Long and Papolis are somewhat extreme examples of differences in behavior, at least among the participants in this study, they are nevertheless representative of the dynamics involved that seem to create those differences. In all fifteen cases, differences in behavior seem to be created both by differences in job demands and by differences in personal characteristics as summarized in Figure 5.1.

In the cases of Long and Papolis, the situations they were in and the demands placed on them were different because of differences in the size of the businesses and organizations involved, differences in the maturity of those businesses, and differences in the type of GM jobs involved. To some degree the individual differences between the two men mirror these differences in their jobs and job contexts. In Richard's case, one might say that he created a context "in his own image." Tom, on the other hand, was selected by others who could point to considerable evidence after a dozen years at IC that he "fit" that context well. Differences in behavior seem to flow from and to be directly related to both these job and individual differences. For example, Richard's informal behavior (dress, use of unscheduled meetings, influence style) flows directly from the small and informal interpersonal context in which he operated and from his strong personal preference for operating that way.

Although they behaved quite differently, both men were performing very well in their jobs. But the data suggests that Papolis was performing somewhat better: excellent versus very good (see Appendix E). This raises one final issue which we have not explicitly addressed: the relationship of differences in behavior and their antecedents to differences in performance.

Differences in Behavior, Their Antecedents, and Performance

As was suggested throughout Chapter 4, the better-performing GMs in this study behaved somewhat differently than the lesser-performing ones. Generally they acted more in accordance with the central tendencies reported in Chapter 4. And more particularly, the excellent performers tended to get information for agenda setting more aggressively and to use it to create more complete (long- and short-term) and more strategic (in a competitive sense) agendas. They also approached network building more aggressively and built stronger networks (better people, better relationships). In execution, they tended to rely on a wider variety of methods, including rather indirect methods, and they spent somewhat less time in that activity (there was less to do since their networks automatically accomplished much and because they were more effective and efficient in getting things done).

In the last chapter we did not explicitly note the antecedents of the different types of behavior associated with different levels of performance, although they could be deduced from the discussion in Chapter 3. To be explicit now, it appears that the greater the gap or misfit between the personal abilities and inclinations of the GM and the demands of his job, the more his behavior will be different in general from that described in Chapter 4, the more it will be specifically different from the excellent performers, and the lower will be his level of performance.

There is an important implication about behavior and performance in this conclusion. That implication can be stated most directly as such: even if an individual knows what behavior is needed for better performance in a GM job, and even if he wants to behave that way, he will probably be unable to do so unless his personal assets fit the job demands in some minimum way when he starts the job.

Gerald Allen's case is particularly interesting in this regard. Allen was one of the two or three brightest managers in this study. He had an MBA and knew a great deal about management; he even occasionally taught management courses at a local college. Allen knew, for the most part, what he should be doing in his job; but he did not behave that way. In particular, he did not spend as much time on agenda setting, especially the longer run and more strategic aspects of it, as he knew he should. He also simply did not build the network that was needed for excellent performance in his job. For example, at least one of the people he inherited as a direct report was hopelessly incompetent, but Allen did not move or fire him. Furthermore, he spent more time in execution, more time doing things himself, and less time using indirect methods to influence others than did the excellent performers.

The way he did behave translated into good/fair performance (see Appendix E), not poor or clearly inadequate; but that kind of performance was certainly below his standards. Shortly after my final meeting with him, he acquired a new boss who (unlike his predecessor) felt that Allen's performance was also below his standards. As a result, he transferred Allen laterally in a move interpreted by some at his bank as a demotion.

To understand Allen's case, we need first to recognize that his background did not conform particularly well to the pattern shown in Figure 3.4 ("Historical Contributions to Fit"). For example, the company he chose to work for fit his values and needs only moderately. He was clearly different from the typical manager in his organization; this was even visually apparent, and Allen was quick to admit it. Early in his career he did not develop a smooth "success syndrome." That is not to say that he wasn't successful early on—he was. But he did not experience the important growth in locally relevant knowledge and relationships that is a central part of that syndrome. In particular, he developed no strong relationships with upper management in his firm.

Allen was promoted to his GM job in 1975 when his predecessor was transfered to another division. At the time, there was no ideal candidate to replace this individual, so he nominated Allen. Taking the job meant a big change for Gerald Allen, since it required that he go from a position where he supervised fewer than a dozen people to one where he would supervise 600; it required that he take on ten times more budgeting responsibility than he had ever had before; and it required that he take responsibility for an area of the bank which was not performing well and had not been performing very well for over a decade. But he felt he had no choice, and he didn't. He could not call on anyone in top management for help or protection.

From all available evidence, Gerald never really got control of the job. He started in over his head and survived only because he was very talented and worked hard. The gap between the network he was able to put together and the short-run agenda imposed on him from above (this was an operations GM job) was so wide that he spent almost all of his time in execution—trying to make up the difference himself. He didn't have time to engage in much agenda setting, he didn't have the resources to build the network he really needed, and his knowledge of what he should be doing did not help a bit.

After examining this case, I can't help but wonder how many other "Allens" there may be in this world which is currently producing more than 60,000 new MBAs each year.

Summary and Discussion

It is not possible, with the small number of cases included in this research, to make any definitive statements about managerial behavior. But it is possible to help disconfirm some popular beliefs. For example, the supposition that all effective managers use essentially the same "style" is simply not supported by the data in this study. The cases of Long and Papolis, and others, clearly show that a great deal of effective managerial behavior is situation-specific. Likewise, the polar opposite proposition—that effective managerial behavior is entirely situation-specific and that no meaningful generalizations are possible—receives no support either. Long, Papolis, and the others did behave in many similar ways, as outlined in the last chapter. Furthermore, the differences in behavior among them can often be predicted from the general model shown in Figure 5.1.

The cases of Long, Papolis, and Allen, and more generally the conclusions we have reached regarding differences in behavior and the factors that create those differences, have powerful implications for a number of areas. In the next chapter, after a brief summary of all the findings for this study, we will explore those implications in some depth.

6

Summary, Discussion, and Implications for Increasing GM Performance

THE INVESTIGATION upon which this book is based was guided by the following questions:

1. *What is the nature of general management jobs today?* What are the key problems, challenges, and demands associated with these jobs? How much and in what way do these demands vary in different situations? What causes this variation?

2. *What kind of people become effective general managers?* What drives them? What skills and abilities do they have? Where have they come from? Why is it that these people have become effective general managers? How much does this all vary in different settings? What causes this variation?

3. *What exactly do effective GMs do?* How do they approach their work? How do they spend their time during the course of a typical day? Why do they behave this way? Why is this behavior "effective"? How much and in what ways does this behavior vary in different settings? Why does it vary?

In a modern "organizational" society, such questions are of more than passing interest. Yet with only a few partial exceptions, they have not previously been addressed through the systematic and in-depth study of a group of successful executives. Such was the launching point of this investigation.

Patterns in the information collected in this study were presented in Chapters 2 through 5. In this chapter, we will first summarize those patterns; then we will explore their implications for increasing GM performance.[1]

Summary

Job Demands

The demands associated with the general-management jobs in this study were large in scope and diverse in character. Key challenges and dilemmas included: (1) setting basic goals, policies, and strategies despite great uncertainties; (2) achieving a delicate balance in the allocation of scarce resources among a diverse set of businesses and functions; (3) keeping on top of a large and complex set of activities to make sure that problems don't get out of control; (4) getting the information, cooperation, and support from bosses to do the job; (5) getting corporate staff, other relevant departments and divisions, or important external groups [unions, big customers] to cooperate; and (6) motivating, coordinating, and controlling a large and diverse group of subordinates. As a result of these demands, the typical GM faced significant obstacles in both figuring out what to do and in getting things done. Indeed, decision making was often extremely difficult because of the great uncertainties involved, the diversity of the issues, and the enormous quantity of potentially relevant information. At the same time, implementation was frequently problematic because of the large and diverse group of people involved and because the job typically supplied relatively little control over those people.

These demands were created both by the very nature of the GM jobs and by the character of the business and corporate contexts in which they were found. The jobs themselves made their incumbents responsible for a number of long-, medium-, and short-run tasks. Specifically, they made the GMs responsible for setting some or all of the basic goals, directions, and priorities for an organization, including deciding what business or businesses to be in, and how to secure key resources; for deciding how to allocate resources effectively to that business or businesses in order to achieve long-run goals; and for the efficient use of the human, financial, and material resources employed in that business or businesses, including some profit responsibility. In addition, these jobs placed the GMs in a web of relationships in which they were made dependent in varying degrees upon superiors, peers, outsiders, and subordinates. Typically they had to report to a GM boss or board of directors, were given some authority over a very diverse set of subordinates, and had to rely on some other internal (such as the corporate staff) or external (such as major suppliers) groups for support, despite the fact that those groups did not report to the GM.

These responsibilities and relationships were imbedded in business and organizational contexts which were often incredibly complex because of the number of people, products, markets, technologies, and countries involved and the uncertainty that was present. Interaction between the job characteristics and these contextual factors produced the complex job demands, made decision making difficult, and created serious implementation problems (as summarized in Figures 2.1 and 2.2, pages 21, 22).

This same type of interaction also produced considerable variety in job demands, both because of large differences among the contexts in the study and because of differences inherent in the way the jobs were defined (Figure 2.3, page 23). Exactly what kind of and how many long-, medium-, and short-run issues were important varied considerably at different sites. Likewise, exactly who (the number, the type of people, their formal relationships) the GM had to work through, and for what, also varied considerably. Overall, the differences in the exact nature and scope of job demands from site to site were significant.

There appear to be at least seven types of GM jobs in existence today. All are characterized by important differences in either their responsibilities or their relationships (see Figure 2.4, page 26). A few of these distinctions are well known today, such as between a corporate CEO's job and an autonomous division president's; most are not. Yet each creates a set of job demands that are different in important ways. Idiosyncracies in the business and organizational contexts in this study created even greater variety in job demands (see Figure 2.5, page 31). Differences in size, age, performance level, product/market diversity, and organizational culture produced an almost limitless variety of contexts; and that in turn produced significant differences in job demands. For these reasons, some general management situations that superficially looked much alike were in fact quite different in terms of the problems and challenges involved, and in terms of the demands made of the general manager.

Furthermore, it would appear that both the variety and the magnitude of the demands associated with GM jobs have been steadily increasing over the last half-century. One of the central trends of our times has been the emergence of the modern corporation, which has continued to grow larger, to take on more diverse products, to include more diverse and geographically dispersed markets, and to incorporate more sophisticated technologies. This fundamental trend is directly linked to the emergence of increasingly varied kinds of general-management jobs, to greater disparities among the contexts in which these jobs are found, to the magnified size and scope of the demands associated with these jobs, and to the considerable diversity we find today among the demands associated with GM jobs. If these and related trends continue (see Figure 2.6, page 31), one can imagine a time when at least some GM jobs will be so demanding that almost no one, not even the most talented and experienced executive, can handle them. And one can imagine a time when the differences between jobs simply overwhelm any similarities.

The Personal Characteristics of Effective General Managers

The individuals in this study all held general-management jobs and were believed to be performing well in those jobs. They were selected to be similar in that regard but in no other. Nevertheless, they turned out to be similar in many other ways as well. Almost all of them were ambitious, achievement oriented, comfortable with power, emotionally stable, temperamentally optimistic, above average in intelligence, moderately strong analytically, intuitively strong, personable, good at developing relationships with people, and able to relate to a broad set of business specialists. They also were very knowledgeable about their businesses and organizations, and had a set of good working relationships with a very large number of people in their companies and in their industries (see Figure 3.1, page 36).

Even more interesting than the specific list of similarities is the fact that these characteristics seem to be related to "core" similarities in job demands across all the situations. It would appear that the reason the GMs were similar in many ways is that their jobs were alike in a number of core ways which required most or all of those characteristics (see Figure 3.2, page 42). Those characteristics seem to have given them both the ability and the inclination to deal with the difficult decision-making and implementation issues associated with their jobs. In a sense, those characteristics appear to fit the key aspects of a GM job in ways that allow a person to both survive and prosper despite difficult job demands.

Similarly, many of the differences among the GMs also appear to be job related, and there were many differences. The GMs were conservative and liberal, big and small, young and old. Some were clearly much smarter than others; some were much more charismatic. At the extremes, the differences seem even greater than the similarities. Yet to a large degree, there was a pattern among these differences; they were often related to differences in job demands (see Figure 3.5, page 54).

In other words, at least a part of the reason that these men were effective in difficult jobs seems to be that they had a large number of personal assets which fit the particular demands of their situations very well. In a sense, therefore, although these successful executives tended to think of themselves as "generalists" capable of managing nearly anything well, they were in fact all quite specialized.

Perhaps even more important, these people-job matches all seem to have had a long history in the making. The many characteristics that appear to have been important in helping these individuals cope with difficult job demands, and even in helping them to get a job that fit them, were developed over a period that spanned their entire lives.

The typical GM was raised in an upwardly mobile, middle-class family which included siblings. The parents, both of whom were at home while he was growing up, had some college education, and the father was usually in business or was a manager in a nonbusiness situation. The GM developed a close relationship with one or both of his parents. In high school and college he became a student leader, and in college or graduate school he concentrated on business or business-related fields. After finishing his education, he quickly settled into an industry and (usually) a company and stayed there. He moved up the hierarchy in one (or two) functions, changed jobs every two or three years, established a strong record of successes, and was promoted into his first general-management job in his late thirties.

This developmental pattern (summarized in Figure 3.3, page 45), sometimes in obvious and sometimes in subtle ways, seems to be directly linked to the key personal assets that were shared by the GMs (see Figure 3.4, page 49). For example, the detailed knowledge they all had of their businesses and organizations and the large numbers of good working relationships they had with people in their companies and industries can be traced to one aspect of the common career pattern: long tenure in one company and one industry. These GMs did not rise in the management hierarchy by changing companies often. Indeed, 91 percent of the typical GM's time in his career was spent in his current industry (broadly defined), and 81 percent of the career time was spent in his current company. As such, it was at least partially through long tenure in a particular situation that they were able to become incredibly knowledgeable about that situation and were able to develop such a large number of good working relationships with other people involved in that situation.

It would thus appear that the development of the large number of special assets required in a GM job simply takes a long time. These successful general managers were not "made" overnight, nor were they simply "born." They were developed over many years. Although this pattern applies to all the GMs in the study, it seems to be especially true of the best performers in the group.

Similarities in the Behavior of Effective General Managers

The key to how these effective GMs mobilized their personal assets to cope with their difficult job demands lies in the creation and use of certain kinds of "agendas" for their businesses and "networks" of relationships in their organizations (and industries).

Armed with a large number of personal characteristics that fit the demands of their jobs, the GMs in this study all approached those jobs in roughly the same way. Initially, they used their current knowledge of the business and the organization, their relationships with relevant others, their native intelligence and interpersonal skills, and other personal assets to learn more about their job's complex demands and to begin creating an agenda for their areas of responsibility. They did so using an ongoing, incremental, largely informal process which involved a lot of questioning and produced a largely unwritten agenda of loosely connected goals and plans (see Figure 4.2, page 66). Concurrent with their initial months on the job, they used those same personal assets to develop a network of cooperative relationships with people, above and below them, inside their organizations and out, upon whom the job and their emerging agenda made them dependent. This was done largely informally, and on a continuous basis, using a wide variety of methods (see Figure 4.4, page 72). After six months to a year, they then began to spend more time focusing on execution—seeing that their networks implemented their agendas (see Figure 4.5, page 75).

In other words, these effective executives did not approach their jobs by planning, organizing, motivating, and controlling in a very formal sense. Instead, they relied on more continuous, more informal, and more subtle methods to cope with their large and complex job demands. The most important products of their approach were agendas and networks, not formal plans and organizational charts. These agendas were not inconsistent with formal plans, but they were different. Agendas tended to cover a wider time frame than did most formal plans; they tended to be less numerical and more strategic in nature; they usually dealt more with "people" issues; and they were typically somewhat less rigorous, rational, logical, and linear in character (see Figure 4.1, page 62). Similarly, their networks were not necessarily inconsistent with the "formal structure," but they were different. They typically included people both inside and outside the firm. These people often had cooperative relationships with the GMs which went far beyond any formal relationships, and groups of these people, especially subordinates, often had informal relationships among themselves that were cooperative in nature, at least with respect to the GM's agenda (see Figure 4.3, page 68).

On a daily basis, this approach manifested itself in a number of common patterns of how the GMs used their time. Specifically, they typically spent the vast majority of their time with other people, discussing a wide variety of topics. In these conversations the GMs usually asked numerous questions, yet they very rarely could be seen making big decisions. These conversations often contained a considerable amount of joking and non-work-related issues. Indeed, in many of these discussions the substantive issue involved was relatively unimportant to the business. The GMs rarely gave orders, but they often tried to influence others. Their time was seldom planned in advance in any detail and was usually characterized by brief and disjointed conversations. All of this took a little less than sixty hours per week.

On the surface, neither this daily behavior nor the general

approach seems very professional. Instead, they seem like inefficient, "seat-of-the-pants" management; but a closer examination suggests otherwise. In looking carefully at how these managers approached their work and at what they did each day, one can see how their behavior flows logically from the real nature of GM job demands and from the type of people one finds in those jobs. And one can see why it works as well as it does (this is summarized in Figure 4.9, page 93).

The way these successful GMs approached their jobs follows directly from the dilemmas and challenges inherent in the job (see Figure 4.6, page 77). For example, because a critical challenge inherent in the job involves getting things done through a large and diverse group of people—including staff that doesn't report to the position, outsiders, subordinates, subordinates of subordinates, bosses—despite having little direct control over most of them, to be successful these GMs had to approach the management functions of staffing and organizing with an eye toward many people besides their direct subordinates. And in doing so, they had to rely on more than formal tools such as structure, selection systems, and compensation systems; they had to rely on a wider range of more informal strategies and tactics. Because of their interpersonal skills, motivation, temperament, knowledge, and relationships, they were able and inclined to do so.

In a similar way, their daily behavior results from the common approach to the job (in conjunction with common job and personal characteristics. See Figure 4.7, page 87, and 4.8, page 91). For example, because the whole approach centers around the development and use of a network of relationships, it is hardly surprising that they spent almost all of their time each day with other people. Although it may not be obvious at first, it can be demonstrated that even a pattern such as engaging in frequent, short, and disjointed conversations is, under these circumstances, understandable, efficient, and effective.

Differences in Behavior

Of course, not all of the GMs behaved in precisely the same ways; there was a wide variety of behavior on some dimensions in terms of exactly how they approached their work and what they did each day. These differences among equally effective managers baffled some of the people who were aware of them; they could not understand how two managers who behaved so disparately could both be effective. Yet these differences are for the most part predictable in light of a realistic appreciation of how unique GM job demands can be (see Figure 6.1, page 132).

Differences in job demands tended to be associated with differences in the personal characteristics of the people found in those jobs, both of which in turn tended to be associated with differences in behavior: the bigger the difference in job demands, the bigger the difference in personal characteristics and in behavior. For example, the GMs in larger contexts tended to have a wider set of cooperative relationships when they started their jobs, tended to build and use greater networks in their approach to the job, and tended to spend more time with people in scheduled meetings on a daily basis.

The forces responsible for these patterns of differences are the same as the forces responsible for creating similarities; these dynamics can be summarized as follows:

1. The behavior of the GMs was shaped by both job and personal characteristics. Knowledge of only one or the other seems insufficient for prediction with any accuracy of how a GM approached the job and what he did each day.
2. Job demands shaped behavior both because they influenced who was selected for the job and because, once in a job, the GMs tended to respond to the job's demands. As such, the same factors which influenced job demands, influenced behavior:
   (a) the type of GM job, or more precisely, the exact configuration of responsibilities and relationships;
   (b) business and corporate factors, such as size, product/market age, performance level, and so forth.
3. Personal characteristics shaped behavior because they represented both what the individual was capable of doing and what the person was inclined to do. These key personal characteristics seemed to include:
   (a) personality factors such as motivation, temperament, cognitive orientation, and interpersonal orientation;
   (b) accumulated business knowledge and relationships.
4. Because there were so many factors involved, these per-

sonal and job characteristics did not combine to shape agenda-setting and network-building behavior in any simple or mechanistic way. But generally,

(a) the nature of the responsibilities and the demands associated with them, the individual's knowledge of the business and organization, and the individual's cognitive orientation all strongly influenced the type of agenda that emerged and the agenda-setting process;

(b) the nature of the job relationships and the demands associated with them, the individual's existing set of relationships, and the individual's interpersonal orientation all strongly influenced the type of network which was created and the network-building process.

5. After the GM had been in the job for a while, the agenda and network that had been created tended also to be critical factors that shaped behavior. The agenda influenced what the GM did (the content of his days) and the network influenced how he did it (the process). For example:

(a) the bigger the network, the less time the GMs tended to spend alone;

(b) the more long-run items (or production items, or whatever) on the agenda, the greater the percentage of their time focused on those items.

Overall, the dynamics summarized here are complex, yet understandable.

The Overall Findings: A Summary Comment

The GMs who participated in this study considered themselves to be "professional" managers. Many had an MBA and all had some formal training in modern management. Yet perhaps the single most fundamental finding arising from this study is that these effective executives were significantly dissimilar in a large number of important dimensions—regarding who they are, what they do, why they behave that way—from the dominant conception today of the effective "professional" manager (see Figure 6.1).

Recently one writer, in an article entitled "The Profession of Management," summarized his interpretation of the professional manager in the following way:

The professional manager in America exists above the industrial din, away from the dirt, noise, and irrationality of people and products. He dresses well. His secretary is alert and helpful. His office is as clean, quiet, and subdued as that of any other professional. He plans, organizes, and controls large enterprises in a calm, logical, dispassionate, and decisive manner. He surveys computer printouts, calculates profits and losses, sells and acquires subsidiaries, and imposes systems for monitoring and motivating employees, applying a general body of rules to each special circumstance. The symbols in which he thinks and works are those of finance, law, accounting, and psychology. Finessed and massaged into ever new formulations, they yield wondrous abstractions. And because the professional manager deals in abstractions, he can move from company to company with relative ease, manipulating people and capital as he goes. Without any abiding commitment to the company, he is a master of the quick fix, yielding the sort of short-term profits institutional investors love.[2]

Although I'm sure that many people, especially executives themselves, would think that this description is silly and obviously not at all related to effective management, it nevertheless is the reigning belief today. Business schools, management-related professional associations, books and journals on administration, and management consulting firms are all—at least to some minimum degree—based on this concept. That is, they all stress universally applicable management knowledge—about formal tools, concepts, and theories—above all else.

The data from this study suggest that, while such knowledge is important, much more is involved in the production of effective executive behavior. A large number of motivational, temperamental, interpersonal, and other personal characteristics are important; experiences, literally starting from birth, are important; some degree of specialization, commitment, and fit with the local environment is important; complex, subtle, and informal behavior are important. All of this is so because of the very nature of executive jobs today.

Implications for Corporate Selection, Development, and Staffing Practices

There are many possible implications from this study for corporate selection, development, and staffing practices. We will focus here on the most obviously important ones.

KEY ISSUES		THE POPULAR VIEW
I. *Who are the effective "professional" executives?*	● What key personal characteristics do they have (which help them do their job)?	● Intelligence, analytical ability, and knowledge of management tools, concepts, theories, etc., are key.
	● How generally applicable or specialized are these characteristics?	● They are broadly applicable.
	● How were these characteristics formed?	● These are developed in adulthood by means of formal training.
II. *What exactly do they do?*	● How do they approach their jobs?	● They create formal plans, structure their subordinates to carry out the plans, and use formal control and reward systems to get plans executed.
	● What does their daily behavior look like?	● They calmly sit in their offices, read reports, analyze data, make decisions, and give instructions to their subordinates.
	● How does this vary in different settings?	● It varies very little in different settings.
III. *Why do they behave this way?*	● Why do we find this pattern of behavior?	● The popular view doesn't speak explicitly to this point.
IV. *Why are some more effective than others?*	● What is the key to excellent performance?	● Good training, knowledge of the latest developments in the science of management, intelligence, and analytical ability.

FIGURE 6.1.   Two views of effective "professional" management

FINDINGS FROM THIS STUDY

- A large number of characteristics are important including ambition, achievement and power motivation, temperamental evenness and optimism, certain types of cognitive and interpersonal skills, detailed knowledge of the business and organization they are in, and many cooperative relationships with other people in that business and organization.

- They are somewhat specialized.

- They developed throughout life—in childhood, via education, and in the early career.

- Initially, they use their many personal assets to create agendas for their areas of responsibility, and networks of cooperative relationships with all those upon whom the job and their emerging agendas make them dependent. They do so using an ongoing, incremental, largely informal process that utilizes many subtle methods. After six to twelve months, they begin to spend more time focusing on execution, in which they get their networks to implement their agendas by directly and indirectly influencing other people.

- They spend the vast majority of time with others (including peers, outsiders, bosses, and subordinates) discussing a wide range of subjects, often in short and disjointed conversations that are not planned in advance in any detail, in which the GMs ask a lot of questions and seldom give orders.

- It can vary a great deal in different settings.

- Because of the nature of executive jobs, which require: (1) decision making in an environment characterized by uncertainty, great diversity, and an enormous quantity of potentially relevant information; and (2) implementation through a large and diverse group of subordinates, peers, bosses, and outsiders, despite having relatively little control over them.

- Having a large number of personal characteristics that fit the complex demands of the job.

Finding GMs: Insiders or Outsiders

The executive search business is booming today,[3] and according to the 1978 Annual Report of the Association of Executive Recruiting Consultants, the most common positions search firms sought to fill in 1978 were general-management jobs. At least 25 percent of all searches were for such jobs. Yet this study suggests that going outside for GMs can be risky; an outsider may be very talented and may have an outstanding track record, but he will rarely have some of the characteristics that are absolutely needed to perform well. Specifically, he will rarely have a detailed knowledge of the business and organization and good, solid relationships with the large number of people upon whom the job makes him dependent. Under certain circumstances, a talented outsider can develop this knowledge and these relationships quickly enough to survive and do well; but most of the time, one probably cannot.[4]

None of the fifteen GMs that were a part of this study (who, on average, performed better than most GMs) were hired into their current positions from the outside. One of them (Firono), however, was hired into a previous GM job from outside his firm. His case illustrates the problem rather clearly. In that job, he made a few strategic errors (by his own admission) because he didn't have time to analyze some options thoroughly. Moreover, he had difficulty implementing his agenda; he met resistance from people whom, by and large, he did not know well. After two frustrating years during which his performance was in the fair-to-good range, he was transferred laterally into his current GM job.

Of course, this does not mean one should never hire executives from outside a firm; instead it suggests that one should try to restrict such hiring to situations where:

- the relevant relations and knowledge can be developed quickly, say in six months (a typical example would be for a small division in a relatively mature industry); or
- where many of the key relationships and knowledge are transferrable across companies (because, for example, it is a mature industry and all businesses are pretty much alike and the key relationships are external, to customers or suppliers); or

- when you're simply desperate and forced to take a risk (such as a turnaround situation).

There is evidence that some corporations have already learned that they must look within for future executives.[5] But in order for this strategy to work, they must have a policy of hiring young managers who can do more than entry-level jobs and who have the potential to fill executive posts in ten to twenty-five years. This in turn will require good business planning, so they will know what kind of businesses will need to be managed in the future; a close linkage between business planning and human-resource planning, so they will know what kind of executives will really be needed in the future; and sophisticated college or MBA recruiting efforts, so they can accurately identify people who have the potential to be the kind of executives they will need. Many leading corporations have already made some real progress on all of these fronts,[6] but most firms I know still have a long way to go.

Developing GMs

In light of the above, this study suggests that firms need to be skilled at systematically developing young managers with high potential after they have been recruited. This means systematically fostering the development of what we have previously called "success syndromes."

An important aspect of the "success syndrome" identified in Chapter 3 is related to growth. The most effective GMs had careers characterized by almost constant growth in their interpersonal and intellectual skills, in their knowledge of the business and organization, and in their relationships with relevant others. They never stagnated for significant periods of time in jobs where there were few growth possibilities. Likewise they were seldom, if ever, moved so often or put into positions that were so rapidly changing that they simply could not learn and perform well. In a sense, they never moved too fast or too slowly.

Moving either too quickly or slowly in a GM career seems to create serious problems. For the very talented, the former is probably a greater cause for concern. Indeed, two of the GMs in this study suffered from moving too quickly. At times during their careers, they were given more and different responsibilities at such a rate that they simply could not learn everything that was necessary or develop all the relationships that they needed. They worked long hours under stress and eventually their performance began to slip.

Moving too slowly can hurt a career in a different way. It appears that if one goes too slowly, he may never get to his desired destination at all. Remember that all but one of the GMs in this study moved into their first general-management jobs before they were forty.

Regulating the speed of a GM career can be as difficult as it is important. Short-run business or corporate pressures often push decision makers to move people too quickly or too slowly. Even GMs themselves sometimes inadvertently accelerate their careers excessively, often because they are unaware of this problem or because they do not know which "speedometer" to watch. The correct index is not (as so many seem to believe) the number of promotions or raises per period of time; nor is it the number of functions worked in or the number of training courses taken. It is something more difficult to measure: growth in interpersonal and intellectual skills, in business and corporate knowledge, and in relevant relationships.

For example, one of the two excellent performers (Poullin) in this study spent the first ten years of his career with his company in essentially three corporate staff jobs. After ten years, he had supervised only a few people, had no line experience, had no direct experience in any of the company's divisions, and had been clearly "promoted" only once. Measured in some conventional ways, this was an incredibly slow period in his career; but measured in terms of growth, it was a moderately fast (but not too fast) period. During this time, he learned an enormous amount about the company and all its divisions. He developed relationships with the president and the rest of top management, and the assignments he was given constantly stretched his skills.

It is even possible for a career experience which looks very slow to be, in fact, too rapid. A young manager I once met complained that his career had come to a dead halt; he had not been promoted in six years. Upon questioning him, I found that he had changed jobs (laterally) three times during this period in a job-rotation program. Each change took him to a different division in his company; the divisions were all in different industries, and one of them was growing (in sales volume) at 60 percent per year. He was trying to convince his management to promote him into a job in yet another division. At the rate he was going, I think he would have physically collapsed before he was forty.

Designing and/or Selecting Training Programs

Perhaps the most important implication from this study regarding training programs, and the role they can play in developing highly effective GMs, is that it may be wise to look closely and carefully before investing much in them. With the possible exception of a few moderately long university-based executive programs, there is no evidence from this study that training programs, after graduate school, played an important role in helping any of the fifteen GMs. Furthermore, the data here strongly suggest that what is taught in many in-house and external programs may simply not be appropriate for executives and people aspiring to executive jobs.

Some of the "time management" programs currently in vogue are a good example of this problem. Based on simplistic conceptions about the nature of managerial work, these programs instruct managers to stop allowing people and problems to "interrupt" their daily work. They tell potential executives that short and disjointed conversations are ineffective. They advise that one should discipline oneself not to let "irrelevant" people and topics get onto one's schedule. In other words, they advise people to behave differently from the effective executives in this study.

This is not to say that training programs cannot play a useful role in the development of effective GMs; they certainly can, but it is a limited role. Later in this chapter I will describe how executive courses at universities can help. Regarding in-house programs, they can probably be of greatest benefit if they are guided by the following kinds of objectives:

- to help participants learn important information that is specifically relevant to the firm and its business and that they are not likely to learn on the job, not generic "knowledge";
- to help participants to develop good relationships with others that will be helpful to them in their jobs in the future, relationships that they are not likely to develop by themselves as a part of their normal routines; and

- to help participants think more systematically about themselves and their own careers, so that they might better manage their own development and work themselves into positions that really fit their capabilities.

Matching People and Jobs

This study strongly suggests that filling a GM job from a pool of people developed internally should involve making a decision regarding whose characteristics best fit the job's demands. Indeed, personnel selection at any level involves matching people with jobs. Richard Papolis put it quite aptly when he told me:

> If a person doesn't fit his or her job, then he has to constantly expend extra energy to get things done right. He has to fight the natural flow, so to speak. This can require a lot of extra effort and it is very inefficient. If the job is a particularly demanding one, even the strongest or most motivated person may not have that much extra energy, and he will thus eventually fail. Such a failure can hurt many people. If the job is not done adequately, all that depend on it can be hurt. And unless the individual really understands that he was in the wrong job in the first place, the blow to his self-esteem can be very damaging.

Only recently have some corporations begun to consider that different types of general-management situations may require somewhat different types of people.[7] Most of the companies in this study did not, although conclusions reported previously support this idea strongly. At least two of the GMs in this study seem to have suffered at some point in their careers because they were in GM jobs that did not fit them; neither performed very well in those jobs.

We have found that the type of GM job, the nature of the business, and the nature of the corporation involved can all shape GM job demands in important ways that can require different kinds of GMs. For example, somewhat different types of people seem to be needed depending upon whether the job context is young or old, small or large, performs well or is in need of a "turn-around."

This study also suggests that matching people and jobs effectively may well involve more than simply selecting someone who fits a job's demands; it may also involve designing jobs so that they fit the characteristics of available job candidates. This might mean structuring things at the top of a company to fit the specific characteristics and experience of the group of executives involved, or it might mean breaking large divisions into two or more parts so that the demands associated with the top jobs in each of the new divisions are more limited, and are thus easier to staff. Or it might mean divesting some divisions, or limiting the diversification strategy so that the top CEO job is a manageable one. I have often wondered, for example, whether the generally lackluster performance of most U.S. conglomerates[8] results from the conglomerate strategy that creates a CEO job with demands which cannot be handled by mortal men.

Implications for Managing General Managers

Good selection and development of GMs and competent staffing of GM jobs, while essential, is still not enough to insure effective performance; the GMs also need to be managed competently. In the short run, poor management of GMs can direct their behavior in ways not associated with good or excellent performance. In addition, poor management of GMs can destroy a success syndrome and squander a rare and valuable resource.

Helping New GMs Get Up to Speed

This study suggests that competent management of GMs begins by helping new general managers get up to speed effectively. Operationally, this means helping them with agenda setting and network building and not diverting their attention elsewhere.

Initially, a new GM usually needs to spend considerable time collecting information, establishing relationships, selecting a basic direction for his area of responsibilities, and developing an organization under him. During the first three to six months, demands from superiors to accomplish specific tasks, or to work on pet projects, can often be counterproductive. Indeed, anything that significantly directs attention away from agenda setting and network building can prove to be detrimental.

In a more positive sense, managers of GMs can probably be most helpful initially if they are sensitive to where the new GM is likely to have problems getting up to speed and to actively aid the GM in those areas. Such areas are often quite predictable; for example, if a person has spent his career going up the ladder in one function and now has been promoted into an autonomous division GM job (a common occurrence, especially in manufacturing organizations), he will probably have serious problems with agenda setting at first because of his lack of detailed knowledge about the other functions that report to him. On the other hand, if a person has spent most of his early career in professional, staff, or assistant-to jobs and is promoted into a GM job where he suddenly has responsibility for hundreds or thousands of people (not an unusual occurrence in professional organizations), he will probably have great difficulty in network building; he doesn't have many relationships to bring with him and he probably is not used to spending time developing a large network. In either case, a GM's boss can be a helpful coach and can arrange activities that foster, instead of retard, the type of actions the GM should be taking.

The Role of Formal Planning and Performance Appraisal

My own observations in this study and elsewhere suggest that the formal planning and performance appraisal systems within which a GM must operate can either significantly help or hinder his performance. As such, they constitute relevant tools for managing or mismanaging GMs, especially in large corporations.

The conclusions in Chapter 4 suggest that a good planning system should help a GM create a workable agenda and a strong network that can implement it. It should encourage the GM to think strategically, to consider both the long- and short-term, and, regardless of time frame, to take into account financial, product/ market, and organizational issues. Furthermore, it should be a flexible tool that the GM can use to help him in network building. It should give the GM leeway and options so that, depending upon what kind of environment he is trying to create among subordinates, he can use the planning system to help achieve that goal.

Unfortunately, many of the planning systems used by organizations in this study, and many others that I have seen over the past decade, do nothing of the sort. Instead, they impose a rigid "number-crunching" requirement on the GM which often does not require much strategic thinking in agenda setting and which can make network building and maintenance needlessly difficult by creating unnecessary conflict among people. I cannot help but wonder whether it would not make more sense to ask GMs for a one-to-five-page statement of their business strategy instead of 100- to 1,000-page "plans."[9]

The discussion in Chapter 2 suggests that a good performance-appraisal system is one that can help a GM focus on the entire job and can help him balance the various aspects of the job appropriately. As was the case with planning systems, it should also be a flexible tool which the GM can use as a part of his network-building activity. Unfortunately, performance-appraisal systems, including those used by a number of the firms in the study, often do neither. All too often they make the balancing act more, not less, difficult by highlighting and rewarding short-run or quantifiable performance only; and by creating conflicts among people, they make network building among subordinates more, not less, difficult.

Allowing Appropriate Differences

Nothing may be more important or more difficult in the management of general managers, especially in large and diverse organizations, than allowing (and even encouraging) different GMs in different contexts to be different.

For many reasons, forces emerge inside all organizations that push for conformity, uniformity, and standardization. This fact of corporate life is not necessarily bad, but these forces can create serious problems insofar as they make the GMs in different contexts behave alike. Chapter 5 rather clearly shows that somewhat different approaches to the job and different daily behavior are needed in different GM situations.

At least two of the GMs in this study were, in my opinion, being managed inappropriately in this regard. They were both in charge of businesses that were significantly different from the "core" of their corporations, yet they were being managed as if those differences did not exist. Pressure was put on them in subtle and not so subtle ways to behave like the rest of the GMs. Both GMs intuitively recognized that those pressures were inappropriate and fought them, but with only limited success and at significant personal cost. I have seen many situations similar to these over the past ten years.

This same type of problem is sometimes associated with age differences. As we saw in Chapter 3, younger GMs tend to be different from older ones in ways that reflect social changes over the past quarter-century. A corporation that does not recognize these inevitable and appropriate differences will tend to mismanage its younger GMs;[10] a few of the companies in this study did just that.

Minimizing the "I Can Do Anything" Syndrome

Because the GMs in this study were so successful, because they often had twenty- or thirty-year track records of win after win, many seemed to have developed an attitude of "I can do anything." As I noted earlier in the book, many of them were surprisingly inarticulate when asked about their strengths and weaknesses; only two of the fifteen gave answers to such questions which seemed to fit the facts I had gathered from talking to others, watching them, from the questionnaire, and so on. Furthermore, when I asked hypothetical questions about the future, most answered in a way suggesting that they thought they could manage anything successfully. Only one was seriously considering some type of big move, but at least hypothetically, most felt they could make a big move and still be very successful. For some, this would be a move to a different company; others felt they could even manage in a different industry. They displayed little conscious awareness of just how specialized their skills, their knowledge, and their relationships really were.

This career problem has two unusual characteristics: It is a "disease" that usually affects only the strong and successful. The person who fails a number of times tends to be forced to recognize that he cannot do everything; in a sense, failure makes him immune to this problem. Second, this disease often remains latent and never creates a serious problem for the victim. It only hurts when a person makes a decision to try to do something in a very different and inappropriate environment—then it can be fatal.

I have seen this same problem affect many of my students over the years. It is often the best who develop it; year after year of straight A's, of scholastic and athletic awards, and of scholarships leaves them with very little sense of who they really are, what they are good at, and what their limitations are. And many of them, like most people, are not inclined to slow down and go through a serious process of self-assessment. As a result, each year I see some very talented young people who are determined to become general managers despite having only a few of the characteristics identified in Chapter 3. And I see others, who probably do have those characteristics, accept jobs in industries or companies that do not seem to fit them at all (usually because that is where they were offered the most responsibility or the most money).

This "I can do anything" syndrome can seriously retard performance and hurt the careers of very talented people; it can kill a "success syndrome." Yet it is a curable disease. Educational institutions can help by encouraging students to assess themselves realistically. But even more to the point, the managers of GMs and potential GMs can be enormously helpful here; through special assignments and their daily interactions, they can either help reduce or magnify this problem.

Implications for Formal Education

A number of universities today claim that, as a part of their mission, they seek to provide training for future general managers and/or to improve the effectiveness of those already in GM jobs. We clearly need such places of higher learning, but a closer look at exactly what most schools do today to fulfill these objectives raises many questions about their effectiveness.

Admissions

One could argue, based on the research reported here, that admissions is as important (if not more so) as the curriculum in the development of future general managers. As we saw in Chapter 3, the characteristics of effective GMs probably begin to develop at birth. By the time they are ready for graduate school, at least fifteen of the twenty-five "common characteristics" of GMs (from Chapter 3) are already identifiable. By the time they might apply to an executive education program, the vast majority of these characteristics are already established. As such, a very important role that educational institutions can play in the development of effective GMs is one of selection; by screening large numbers of people on relevant dimensions and admitting those who have a reasonably high probability of becoming effective GMs, educational institutions can provide an invaluable service for corporations, for individual managers, and for society in general.

It is not at all obvious, however, that most educational institutions are providing this very valuable service today. Instead, far too many appear to screen young applicants to MBA programs almost solely on test scores and college grades; they do so despite previous evidence that those criteria alone do not correlate with future success in management.[11] Some of the newer schools offering MBA degrees seem to select people based only on their ability to pay for the program. Much (if not most) of executive education appears not to select at all. Anyone who can pay the fee is admitted.

More effective and more useful admissions policies are possible today. But for most business schools, this will require more attention and resources than are currently devoted to admissions; and it will require additional research, which almost all schools are capable of doing, on the relationship of admissions criteria, performance in the curriculum, and career results.

The Curriculum

Furthermore, if one examines the curriculum associated with most general-management programs, one finds other problems. This study suggests that a GM curriculum should focus on:

- both the intellectual and interpersonal aspects of the job;
- intuitive as well as analytical skills;
- long-, medium-, and short-run activities/tasks/responsibilities;
- up, down, and lateral relationships;
- what managers really do and why;
- why some GMs are more effective and satisfied than others; and
- how this differs in different settings.

Few programs seem to deal with more than half this educational agenda.

The intellectual aspects of management are usually stressed at the expense of the interpersonal. Analytical skills are generally developed while intuitive skills are ignored. Medium- and short-run activities and responsibilities are often stressed without adequate attention to the long run. Downward relationships are explored while lateral ones are neglected and upward ones are often ignored. What managers should do (someone's theory) is discussed instead of what good managers actually do. Satisfaction is seldom seriously explored. Situational differences are often largely ignored.

Many of these deficiencies are correctable today; other deficiencies will require more research or thought. For example, I'm not sure we really know how to teach effectively about some of the interpersonal aspects of the job, or about intuitive skills, although we have recently increased our understanding of these areas.[12]

It is, of course, possible that some areas such as intuitive skills are not teachable; but that does not mean that they should be ignored. If they are not teachable, then those qualities should be a part of the admission criteria. Somehow, they should be systematically taken into account.

Career Management

Educational institutions can help GMs or potential GMs become more effective by exposing them to the types of ideas discussed here and by helping them learn to use these ideas in managing their own careers. More specifically, educational institutions should be able to help students:

- assess whether they really have the qualities associated with effectiveness in general management;
- move into a company and industry that fits them;
- create a "success syndrome" in their career development; and
- approach a GM job (when they get one) in an effective way.

But if we look at what schools are currently doing, there seems to be a significant gap between today's reality and what is needed.

Most educational institutions still assume that career management is entirely the student's own problem or concern; it is treated as a "nonacademic" issue that is not worthy of faculty attention or resources. Furthermore, when help is given, it is often based on someone's model of how things might or should work, or on yesterday's realities.

Helping students increase their ability to assess themselves and manage their own career development is possible today. It is even possible to do this within a regular academic format—a rigorous course, taught by a member of the faculty to classes of from thirty to seventy-five people. I have had nearly ten years of experience with such a course[13] and am most impressed by the results.

Broadening Perspectives

Because the GMs in this study tended to specialize in a company and an industry in order to help them cope with their difficult job demands, they faced an important occupational hazard. Since they were exposed to a limited set of stimuli over the years, even the brightest and most capable of them could easily form many opinions, conclusions, and generalizations which were simply false. It was easy for them to develop parochial beliefs and tunnel vision.

This tunnel vision was perhaps most evident in the cases of the older GMs in older companies. These men often accepted some critical factors in their situations as fixed, even though they were not (for example, the business strategy), or held uninformed ideas about other factors they did try to manipulate (such as organizational structure). As a result, in their approaches to their jobs, they often did not create a realistic business strategy as a part of their agendas, or a strong organization as a part of their networks.

Educational institutions can play an invaluable role in helping GMs avoid this problem. They can do so by:

- bringing together people from very different business and corporate settings;
- exposing them to a wide variety of issues, possibilities, and ideas; and
- challenging people's conclusions, ideas, and opinions.

I am not at all sure that the most popular form of executive education can fulfill this important role. Two- or three-day seminars, often in an executive's own city, are simply too short to expose people to much or to chip away seriously at existing conclusions. They also tend to attract too homogeneous a clientele.

Longer programs that include a diverse group of people and that are demanding can help, but there is a tendency on the part of many corporations and executives to shy away from such programs. Longer programs are often seen as expensive and disruptive to both the company and the person's family. This tendency is understandable, but regrettable and shortsighted.

Implications for Management Theory and Research

If not immediately, surely over the long haul, better management theory and research can also help improve the performance of general managers. This study suggests a number of implications for the development of such theory and research.

Key Implications for Managerial Behavior Theory

Theories of management behavior, at least as I shall define them, are explicit and interrelated sets of beliefs about (a) what managers actually do (i.e., the real nature of managerial work); (b) how much and in what ways this varies in different situations (i.e., how managerial work differs in different kinds of managerial jobs or in different contexts); (c) why managers behave as they do (i.e., how individual and contextual factors shape behavior); and (d) what impact that behavior has (i.e., why some are more "effective" than others, why some are more personally satisfied than others).

This study suggests that sound theories of managerial behavior should have, at a minimum, the following characteristics:

- They must include at least four classes of variables—individual (personal and background characteristics); contextual (job, business, organization); behavioral; and effectiveness (some performance measures). The fact that most of the early work in the area of managerial behavior produced either contradictory or uninteresting results is directly linked to missing classes of variables in the theories that directed such work. In particular, by ignoring context, early work that tried to identify the individual characteristics of managers,[14] to correlate individual characteristics and performance,[15] and to correlate behavior (style) and performance,[16] achieved very litte.

- Sound theories must recognize that the context in which at least some managers work is very complex and can vary significantly in many dimensions in different situations. One of the key reasons that the vast amount of leadership research conducted in this century adds up to so little is probably because it has been guided by theories that, even when context is taken into account, treat context in incredibly simplistic ways.[17]

- Within the class of individual variables, good theories must include a wide range of background and historical variables. Theories that ignore or discount history almost inevitably lead to inaccurate conclusions about change and dynamics. Probably one of the key reasons that research on management training programs has often suggested that they produce little if any change[18] is that such programs are based on an ahistorical, "here and now," theory of managerial behavior.

- In terms of behavior, adequate theories must include variables, concepts, and relationships that deal with both decision making and implementation, with both subordinate-manager interaction and manager-other interaction—that is, with all relevant aspects of behavior. Another reason why early work on managerial behavior achieved limited results was that it was guided by theories that focused attention almost exclusively on very limited aspects of behavior, such as manager-subordinate interaction.[19]

- Also in terms of behavior, sound theories must include concepts for behavior in different time frames (during one year, or in twenty-four hours) and be explicit about that. One of the key reasons why recent observational work on managerial behavior and more traditional management theories have been difficult to reconcile is that they tend to focus (implicitly) on behavior in different time frames. The newer work deals with daily behavior, the more traditional work with behavior in much longer time frames.

Key Implications for Research Topics

By design, this was not a study that could "prove" something. The number of participants was limited, and despite great effort to avoid biases, the methods for selecting participants and gathering data have their obvious limitations. What this study does do is generate ideas—about relevant variables and relationships— which can be pursued with future research.

Of the many questions that could be included in research projects on managerial behavior, this study suggests that the following are among the most important:

- What kind of responsibilities, relationships, and job demands are associated with various types of managerial jobs (e.g., in marketing and finance, at middle and lower levels)? How are they similar or different to GM jobs and to each other?
- Are size, product/market age, and performance level the most important contextual factors that create differences in job demands among the same kinds of jobs in different settings? Or are other factors, such as product/market diversity or culture, more important?
- How much do the personal characteristics of effective managers in different kinds of managerial jobs vary? Is the list we found in this study generally applicable for all GMs?
- Precisely how do the important personal characteristics of effective managers develop over time? How relatively important are childhood, educational, and early career experiences? Are the important developmental dynamics different for successful managers in different kinds of managerial jobs? Or for women?
- How exactly do successful managers think, make decisions, and create agendas? What goes on in their minds? What kind of conscious and unconscious processes are involved? Does this vary significantly among successful managers in different types of jobs, or in different settings? Why?

- Do the strategies and tactics managers employ to develop and use networks vary much in different settings or jobs? If yes, how and why is this so? Also, are certain personal skills, abilities, and inclinations closely related to the use of certain strategies and tactics?
- Can any daily behavior pattern be predicted by single contextual or personal variables alone, or must one always take into account interaction effects and intervening factors?

Key Methodological Implications

A greater concern with the kind of questions listed above will require more longitudinal, historical, and multiple-method field research, and it will require less emphasis on the single most popular research method in use today—the single questionnaire. Unfortunately, shifting our emphasis from research based on a single questionnaire to work based on longitudinal, historical, and multi-method field based studies will not be easy.

I have recently reread the Appendix to William F. Whyte's *Street Corner Society*. I am struck by the similarities in his and my field experiences, despite the fact that we were studying radically different groups of people (Whyte was focusing on lower-class men, often unemployed, in an Italian-American slum community) at very different times (Whyte's work was done in the 1930s) and despite differences in the scope of our studies (his was larger and took more time). I think these commonalities—the major ones which I will discuss here—say something important regarding field research studies, why we see so few of them, and what will be required to break away from our reliance on single-shot questionnaires.

First of all, field research tends to be very time-consuming. Whyte worked in the field nearly full time for two years during a study that absorbed about four years from start to finish. I spent over two years on a part-time basis gathering data in a study that will require five years from beginning to end. These experiences are not unusual.[20]

Young researchers tend to lack the time or the incentive to undertake long projects. The reward systems in academia, much like the reward systems in business organizations, tend to be biased toward the more measurable short run. An assistant professor who invests all his time in a field study will not, when he is reviewed for promotion to associate, have the list of publications that is prerequisite for advancement at most universities.

Older researchers, such as tenured academics, can do field research without risking career progress. But few do because, by the time they have tenure, they have made commitments which require most of their energy. They typically have teaching commitments, administrative commitments, consulting commitments, and family commitments. Unlike young Bill Whyte, they cannot just pick up and spend a few years working full time on a field study. Furthermore, I think they are less inclined to put up with the pain and suffering that they would have accepted earlier in their lives.[21]

A second, related reason why so few field studies are conducted has to do with the problem of getting access to a site and gaining the cooperation of the people involved. Gaining access and cooperation can be very difficult and time consuming; it is infinitely easier to get a group of students or lower level employees to spend fifteen to sixty minutes filling out a questionnaire than it is to do the typical field study. The former requires little effort from an easily accessible group; the latter requires considerable effort and commitment, often from a much less accessible group. As such, successfully gaining such access and commitment requires time and resources as well as certain attitudes and skills, but many researchers just do not have these.

The primary skills that most researchers have are associated with thinking—an ability to conceptualize, an ability to be precise and critical, an ability to be rigorously logical. People are usually not selected into research roles because of their skills at interpersonal influence, yet it is precisely those skills that are needed by the field researcher.

Nor are useful influence techniques usually a part of graduate social science education. Even in a school as devoted to field research as Harvard Business School, we do not always systematically instruct our graduate students in methods of gaining access and commitment. Nor have I ever seen a standard research methods text which adequately discusses such basic issues as:

- the key role a respected leader can play in a field study. Whyte talks about how one person, Doc, was able to get him the access he needed. Even he was surprised at this. "At the time I found it hard to believe that I could move in as easily as Doc had said and with his sponsorship. But that indeed was the way it turned out."[22] My own experiences confirm this; when a respected GM said I was OK, I was in.

- the role of "logical explanations" and relationships. Whyte concluded that his "acceptance in the district depended on the personal relationships I had developed far more than upon any explanation (of the research) I might give."[23] Again, my experiences were similar. I found I sometimes lost access to a site or someone's help by trying to explain logically (as I would to a faculty colleague) the research I was doing.
- the importance of patience and the problems that can be caused by asking too direct a question too quickly. Whyte reports that an important lesson from Doc was worded: "Go easy on that 'who,' 'what,' 'why,' 'when,' and 'where,' stuff, Bill. You ask those questions and people will clam up on you. If people accept you, you can just hang around, and you'll learn the answers in the long run without even having to ask the questions."[24] Again, this fits my experience.

Furthermore, gaining access and cooperation requires not only skill but attitudes that allow one to relate to the people he or she is studying. It is obvious that Bill Whyte truly liked many of the people he describes in his book and that he worked at relating to them.[25] I suspect my feelings about the majority of the managers in the study are just as obvious. Yet, not infrequently, academic researchers do not like or trust managers (or any people in positions of power). These feelings show and inhibit their ability to do research on such people except from a distance (through questionnaires only, or from data collected by others).

A third problem that limits the amount of field research done, in addition to issues of time and access, is that such research cannot be done in a clean way that fits traditional notions of "science." For example, traditional notions of science suggest that in good research the researcher does not influence the object of the research, except as a part of a planned and controlled experiment. The thought of collaborating with the object of the study, as Whyte did with Doc to help him in his analysis[26] (and as I have done), is considered preposterous. Furthermore, scientific research is supposed to occur in a clearly planned sequence; field research tends to be much more fluid. Whyte reports that the purpose of his study shifted over time,[27] and that data gathering and analysis were highly intertwined.[28] I have found the same to be true in my work. As a result of these and other issues, researchers shy away from "unscientific" field research.

Overall, there are many reasons why we do not see more field research done in the social sciences; many of the same forces restrict longitudinal and historical research. If we are to make real progress on the list of research questions presented in this chapter, and if we are to develop the kind of theories this study suggests, we *must* find ways to overcome these obstacles. The challenge is certainly significant, but then, so are the stakes involved.

Appendix A _____

The Study

THE OVERALL PURPOSE of this investigation was rather broad. It was originally guided by the following types of questions:

- What are general-management jobs really like? What demands do they make of the incumbent GM? How much and in what ways do these demands vary in different kinds of GM jobs and in different business and corporate contexts? What creates this variation?
- What type of people tend to be effective in GM jobs? How can such people be identified? Why are these people effective in GM jobs? How much and in what ways do the personal characteristics of effective general managers vary in different situations? What causes this variation?
- What exactly do effective general managers do? How do they approach their jobs? What do they do on a daily basis? Why do they behave this way? How much and in what ways does all this vary from situation to situation? What causes these differences?

Guided by these questions, this was first and foremost a study of people in certain kinds of jobs. It was not, strictly speaking, a study of management or general management, since the latter tends to be defined in terms of tools (e.g., industry and competitive analysis), concepts (e.g., strategy), or principles (e.g., span of control). Of course, the findings are of considerable relevance to these and other managerial topics, but those topics were not the central focus here. Likewise, this was not a study of all kinds of managers; the focus was narrower than that, although many of the findings may be applicable—the reader can judge for himself—to a wide range of managerial and professional jobs in modern organizations.

The research design chosen to answer such questions was based on my own interpretations of prior research on managers[1] and by my own work during the 1970s.[2] This design called for the collection of considerable information on the very nature of the GM jobs, on the background and personality of each manager, on the GMs' on-the-job behavior, and on the impact of that behavior (results). It required a wide variety of methods to gain this information, including observation, interviews, questionnaires, and the collection of relevant documents.[3]

The Process of Inquiry

Access was gained to the participants in the study through a letter to the heads of their corporations. A total of twelve such letters were sent, only three companies refused. When that access was granted, I worked with a company official to select and approach one, two, or three of their GMs. When a GM agreed, an introductory meeting of one or two hours was arranged to discuss details of the study, to obtain some general information on his situation, and to work out the logistics of how we would proceed. At that meeting I also asked for written information about his job, company, and industry; this information typically took the form of an organization chart, product brochures, a one- or five-year plan for his business, and magazine articles or books about the company, the industry, or the general manager himself.

Sometime between one and three months later, the GM was visited again, but this time for three entire days. Before this visit, I studied all the information already collected from that particular GM; during the visit, I spent most of the time simply observing and taking notes on what I saw and heard. Wherever the GM was, I was there taking notes. If the GM was in a formal meeting in a conference room, I was included. If he was just sitting at his desk reading his mail, I was there too. Even when he flew to another city on business, I went with him. When not observing, I interviewed for thirty to sixty minutes each of the key people with whom the GM worked (usually about ten subordinates, bosses, and peers) and the GM himself (see Appendix B for the interview guides). In most cases the GM was interviewed on several occasions, adding up to a total of three or four hours. In a few cases, I also spent an evening with the GM and his wife. At the end of this visit, the GM was given two questionnaires to fill out and mail to me at his leisure (see Appendix C).

Between four and seven months later the GM was visited again for one-and-a-half to two days. Before this visit, I reviewed the question-naires and the information from my previous visit. This third visit was much like the second one except that "key people" were not formally interviewed unless particular individuals had been missed; I simply ob-served and interviewed the GM. At the end of the visit, a copy of a dozen or so pages from a typical period in his appointment book was usually obtained.

After the final visit, all the information collected was organized and studied. Then a brief summary description of the situation was written.

An Example of the Methodology in Action

The process used to study the GMs varied only slightly from individ-ual to individual: for example, in the case of John Thompson it worked as follows:

In June of 1978 a letter was sent to the president of John's bank asking for the bank's participation in this study. A copy of that letter is shown in Figure A.1. A bank was chosen because financial service insti-tutions are a large part of our economy today. John's particular bank was chosen because it had some ties to Harvard and probably valued maintaining good relations with the school (hence might be more willing than the average bank to participate in the study).

Two months after sending the letter, I received a call from a corpo-rate personnel manager who said that the bank had tentatively agreed to be involved (some corporations responded more quickly, perhaps within two weeks; others responded even more slowly, taking up to four months). He wanted to talk with me, so we met in his office a few weeks later. I assumed the primary purpose of this meeting was to test my credibility and behaved accordingly. During the meeting I answered his questions about the study, then we selected two GMs at the bank for possible participation. The criteria employed were: (a) that they be in different parts of the bank (retail versus commercial finance); (b) that they might be inclined to agree to be studied; and (c) that their bosses might be inclined to agree also. Two weeks after this meeting, the per-sonnel officer called to inform me that one of the two GMs had agreed to participate and that the other, John, had tentatively agreed, subject to meeting with me.

I called John in September and set up a short meeting at his office. Again, I assumed my credibility was the key issue here. At the meeting we chatted for about one half-hour, after which he agreed to partici-pate. I then asked him some broad background questions about himself (job history, current family situation) and his business (size, products), and worked with him to identify what written information was available

Dear

    The Division of Research at Harvard Business School has funded a three year study, under my direction, of managers in general-management positions. This investigation will take a very close look at about fifteen general managers in terms of who they are, how they approach their jobs, exactly what they do on a daily basis, what problems they encounter, and how they cope with their problems. Our objective is to increase significantly what we know about the demands and parameters of general-management jobs, the types of people who perform well in those jobs, the concrete behaviors that are needed to deal effectively with those jobs, and how this all varies in different corporate and business settings.

    I would very much like to explore the possibility of inviting two or three of your general managers to participate in this study. Their involvement would require my visiting them for two days on three different occasions over a six month period in order to talk to them, to observe them in their jobs, and to briefly interview those with whom they work closely. My summary observations about each manager would be provided to the manager, and our conclusions from the overall study would be available to all participants and participating organizations.

    Please let me know by letter or phone (617/495-6373) if we might get together briefly to explore who in your organization might be appropriate for this study. At that time I could also answer any of your questions about the details of the study. If we agreed to proceed, I would then contact the selected managers to solicit their involvement.

    If the school is to provide leadership to the business education community, we must depend upon the generous support of people like yourself. We do hope you can help.

                                Yours very truly,

FIGURE A.1. The letter used to solicit interest in the study

that might be of use to me. We subsequently found a number of product brochures, an annual report of the bank, and a few other documents. At the end of the meeting we agreed to begin the work in the spring of 1979.

In January of 1979 a three-day visit was scheduled for February. His secretary set up thirty- to sixty-minute meetings with about eight other people at the bank, including his boss, his immediate subordinates, and one other person with whom he worked closely. In scheduling the meetings I gave him three criteria: (1) no meetings, or a minimum of meetings, on the first day so that I could get a feeling for the situation before having to interview people; (2) not more than three meetings back-to-back, to prevent interviewing fatigue; and (3) no meeting while John had something obviously important on his schedule. In preparation for the visit, I studied all the documents I had previously received from John.

I flew to New York on February 5th and stayed in a hotel that evening. I arrived at the bank the next morning at about 8:25 A.M.; John arrived at 8:30, followed closely by Jim Larson, one of his subordinates. John introduced me to Jim and then they talked for about fifteen minutes; I settled into a chair in his office and took notes on their conversation. When Jim left, John briefly described what was on his calendar for the day and then went to work looking through a pile of papers on his desk. In this case, and whenever John was not talking with someone, I used the time to fill in holes in my notes. For example, at that time I drew a diagram of his office, noting the size, decoration, seating arrangement, etc. At 9:05 John asked Jean Palmer, his secretary, to do a few specific things for him, and at 9:10 he received a phone call. At 9:15 he called Bud Carson, an accounting staff person, into his office to review a report on fourth-quarter results which Bud was preparing. At 9:20, Bud left and Tony Brown, one of John's subordinates, came in. They talked briefly about Tony's health, and then John raised two issues with him. At 9:30 Tony left.

The day continued in a similar manner. John went about his work; I took notes. Whenever John encountered someone I had not met before, he introduced me, varying the nature of the introduction depending upon the person involved (generally with a peer or boss he spent more time explaining who I was). The major events of the day included a meeting on the status of all "problem" loans, a one-hour monthly meeting of his entire staff, and a special meeting to focus on marketing solutions to boost sagging revenues in one area. By the end of the day (5:30), I was on page fifty in my notebook.

I arrived the next day at about 8:30, as did John. We chatted briefly about the events of the previous day until a telephone call directed his attention elsewhere. In addition to being with John, on this day I spent nearly four hours interviewing others at the bank. I used an empty office for most interviews, and generally found the people to be very pleasant and candid. I asked each of them about themselves, their jobs, the bank, and the division, as well as about John, his behavior, and his effectiveness as a manager. Major events in John's day included a meeting with one of the bank's clients, a meeting on a problem loan, and a discussion about an employee who was not performing well. By 5:15, I again had taken about fifty pages of notes.

The third day was much like the second. At the end of the day, I gave John two questionnaires. One solicits facts about a GM's family background, education, and career history as well as information regarding his satisfaction with his job, career, employer, lifestyle, and family. The other asks questions about personal preferences—likes and dislikes, attitudes and values (see Appendix C). I asked him to fill out these questionnaires and to mail them to me within the next few months.

At the beginning of May, I called John and scheduled two days in June for my third and final visit. Immediately prior to this visit, I reviewed the questionnaires John had returned as well as my notes from the first two visits. When I arrived on June 18, we spent nearly an hour talking about what had been happening at the bank since my last visit. During these two days, we managed to squeeze into his schedule nearly three hours for me to interview him; I asked him a broad range of questions about his background, his career, his approach to his job, his business, his organization, and the job itself. The rest of the time was much like the first day of my previous visit; I followed him from meeting to meeting, encounter to encounter. Near the end of the second day, he asked me if I had any observations to make regarding what I had seen. I volunteered a few, and we discussed them. In return, I asked for and received copies of a dozen pages in his appointment book. I thanked him for all his help, promised to keep him informed of the progress of the study, and left.

The Process in Retrospect: A Few Reflections

With only a few exceptions,[4] this process left me with the same types of information concerning all fifteen GMs. The information came from multiple sources, so validity could be checked and "playing to the camera" could be recognized. It covered a wide territory: there was information on their backgrounds, personalities, behaviors, performances, and aspirations as well as on their jobs, organizations, businesses, and industries (see Figure A.2). Overall, I ended up with files on each manager that were four to eight inches thick.

Data Collection Methods

1. Interviews with the GMs—nearly 100 hours in all
2. Interviews with the others with whom they worked—nearly 200 people in all
3. Observation of the GMs in action—well over 500 hours in all
4. Collection of relevant written documents (five-year plans, job descriptions, appointment books, annual reports, etc.)—about 5,000 pages of material
5. Questionnaires—two filled out by each GM

The Content of the Data Collected

1. On the GMs' background
2. On their personal characteristics
3. On their jobs
4. On the business and organizational contexts
5. On their behavior
6. On the results of that behavior

The Relationship of Sources to Content

Source \ Type of Data	Background	Personality	Job and Its Context	Behavior	Results
Questionnaires	**	**		*	*
Observation		*	*	**	*
Appointment Diary				*	
Interviews With Others	*	**	**	**	**
Interviews with the Manager	**	*	*	*	*
Available Printed Information			**		**

Key: ** = a primary source
* = a secondary source

FIGURE A.2.   A summary of the process of inquiry

The most difficult aspect of the process, at least for this researcher, related to stamina. Keeping up with these managers during what were often long days was sometimes very difficult. This was made particularly hard by the nature of the role I played; on some days, a hundred pages of notes were taken.

Gaining access to these managers, although very time-consuming, was not as difficult as I had originally feared; I was turned down by only a few people or companies. Being readily accepted as an observer and interviewer was more difficult, but manageable; the key was gaining the trust of the general manager. As long as the GM made it clear that I was "all right," others generally treated me as one of them. Convincing the GMs to allow me to be with them at all times required effort but was not a problem; only three of the fifteen GMs would not allow me to attend all their meetings. In one case I was shut out of two meetings, in the second case four, and in the third only one. Invariably these were meetings with their bosses.

The final visit with the last GM was in August 1979. Shortly thereafter the slow and often tedious process of sifting through the enormous amount of information collected began. This process required nearly two years.

Appendix B _____

Interview Guides

For Associates of the GMs

PEOPLE OTHER THAN the general managers were usually interviewed for one hour each. The questions they were asked tended to be the following:

1. What is your background? How long have you been with the company? How long have you known the general manager? What are the biggest problems or challenges you currently face in your job?
2. What are the key things one needs to understand about this business and this organization if he is truly to understand the context in which the general manager works?
3. What are the key things he has done, good or bad, in his job? Why did he do that? What impact did it have?
4. How do you normally interact with him? How often? Why? What does he do? Examples?
5. How would you describe him as a manager and a person?
6. How would you rate his performance? Why?

For the General Managers

The general managers were generally interviewed on three to five occasions for a total of four or five hours. The questions they were asked were:

1. Describe the key characteristics of the business you are in.
2. Describe your organization.
3. Describe your job. Being very effective in this job means what?
4. Chronologically, what are the key things that have happened since you took this job? What did you do? Why? What effect did it have? What problems developed? How did you handle these problems?
5. What are the toughest decisions you have had to make in the last few years?
6. What were the high and low points in your life over the past few years?
7. How effective do you think you have been in this job? Specifically why do you say this? Performance measures? What is it about you, the job, or its context that has contributed to this level of effectiveness? Where could you have done better? Why didn't you?
8. How would you describe your managerial style? How has it changed over the past five to ten years (if at all)?
9. What are you trying to achieve in your career? In your life?
10. For events observed during the day: What exactly were you trying to do when you . . . ? Why were you trying to do this? Why did you do it the way you did?
11. How typical or unusual were the events observed?

Appendix C _____

Questionnaires

Two QUESTIONNAIRES were used in the data-gathering process. One was a standard instrument, the other was created specifically for this study.

The Strong-Campbell

All of the GMs in the study filled out an instrument known as the Strong-Campbell Interest Inventory (SCII). The SCII contains more than 300 questions that elicit personal preferences (likes, dislikes, or indifferences) concerning various occupations, school subjects, activities, amusements, and types of people. The test's input, therefore, is data about what we generally call "interests" or "attitudes." The SCII does not elicit information regarding a person's intelligence, aptitudes, or skills.

The instrument uses this information about a person's interests to compute a number of "scores" which are generally presented in three parts: (1) General Occupational Themes; (2) Basic Interest Scales; and (3) Occupational Scales. Each of these three sets of scores compares the test taker's interests with either men or women in general or with men and women in specific occupations such as bankers or advertising executives.

The Occupational Scales

The occupational scales have been created to inform the taker how similar his or her interests are to the interests that are somewhat idiosyncratic to a particular male or female occupational group (such as female bankers or male engineers). Specifically, each of the over 100 occupational scales was created in the following manner:

1. A group of about 150–450 men or women were identified as being happily employed in an occupation and as having been in that occupation for more than three years (average tenure was usually ten to twenty years).

2. These people were asked to answer the 325 questions on the SCII.

3. Whenever these people expressed some particular preference much more often or much less frequently than a large sample of "people in general," that alternative was used in creating the scale for that occupational group.

4. The scale was then normed so that the average person in the occupational group scored 50[1] on the scale while two-thirds of the group scored between 40 and 60.

As a result of this scale-construction procedure, the more often a person using the SCII expresses preferences that distinguish a particular occupation, the greater the score he or she will receive on that occupational scale. For example, suppose a person indicates in response to question 217 that he or she liked "living in the city." Suppose also that the criterion group of male architects happened to choose that option much more often than did most people. In that case, that person's score on the M architect scale would go up a notch. If time and again he or she chose options that had been chosen by male architects (liking, disliking, or being indifferent to an item) but not chosen by others, then the final score on the M architect scale would probably be high, usually considered to be a score of 45 or above. That person and the criterion group of architects are indicating shared attitudes; they have something in common, they express similar preferences.

Sharing a large number of preferences with people in an occupation is important because research has linked such commonalities to people's decisions to go into and stay in an occupation.[2] It would appear that, given an appropriate level of ability, those who tend to share the same preferences as other occupation members—those who "talk the same language"—are also more likely to get on, to be readily accepted, to enjoy their work, and to be successful.

Other Scales

The SCII provides other data besides the occupational scale scores. There are basic interest scale scores, general occupational theme scores, and a few other specialty scale scores. I have found these scores to be less revealing, and thus less interesting, than the occupational scale scores. For a more complete explanation of these scores and the overall test, see *Manual for the Strong-Campbell Interest Inventory* (Stanford, Cal.: Stanford University Press, 1974).

The Background Questionnaire

Each of the GMs also filled out a background questionnaire. An exact replica of that questionnaire follows.

STRICTLY CONFIDENTIAL

GENERAL MANAGER RESEARCH PROJECT
BACKGROUND QUESTIONNAIRE

Harvard Business School
Fall 1977

Instructions: Please answer all the questions completely. Feel free to write in the margins to clarify your answers if necessary. This should require approximately thirty minutes to complete.

1. Birthdate: _____ _____ _____
                     month   day   year

   Birthplace: _____ _____ _____
                     city   state   country

2. Parents: *Mother*   *Father*

   • Living? (if not, date of death)   _____ _____
   • Education (highest grade
     completed, or degree received)   _____ _____

   • Occupation   _____ _____

   • Religion   _____ _____
   • How much influence did each
     parent have in your home while
     you were growing up?   _____ _____
   • How close did you feel to each
     parent when growing up?   _____ _____

3. Brothers and Sisters: (Note if any of them are half- or step-)

   Name   *Age*   *Educational Background*   *Occupation*

   _____   ____   _____   _____

   _____   ____   _____   _____

   _____   ____   _____   _____

   _____   ____   _____   _____

   _____   ____   _____   _____

   _____   ____   _____   _____

4. Home: In what city or cities did you live while growing up (until age 18)?

Approximately when did you live in each city?

City　　　　　　　　　　　　　　　　　　　　　*Dates*

_____　　　　_____

_____　　　　_____

_____　　　　_____

_____　　　　_____

5. Education:

	High School	*College*	*Graduate School*
Name			
Major area of study			
Approximate standing in class			
Extracurricular activities (include positions held)			
Awards, honors, etc.			

6. Occupational History:

  • Describe any part time work while in school.

  • Have you served in the Armed Forces? If yes, indicate dates, branch, and ranks.

  • Full time employment:

  Approximate Dates   *Employer*   *Job Description*

7. Personal Health: What serious illnesses, accidents, or operations have you had in the past? Are you currently being treated by a physician? If yes, for what?

8. Your family:

   • Married? (If yes, give date of marriage)_____

   • Is this your first marriage?_____

     (If not, give dates of other marriages)_____

   • Children? (If yes, give sex and ages)_____

   _____   _____

   _____   _____

   • Please describe your wife's full- or part-time employment outside the home, if any.

9. Nonwork Activities: How do you spend your time off the job? (Be sure to include a description of any hobbies, or organizations you belong to.)

10. Commuting:

   • Where do you live?   _____
   • How far is this
     from work?   _____
   • How do you
     generally get to
     and from work?   _____
   • How long does it
     usually take to get
     to your office?   _____

11. Your current job:

    • As specifically as possible, what are you held responsible for in your current job?

    • What formal authority is inherent in the job?

    • On the average, how many hours per week do you work (including work done at home)?

    • On the average, what percentage of your working time is spent alone?

    • On the average, how many days per month do you travel overnight away from home because of your work?

12. General:

- How happy are you currently with (circle one number for each question)?

	extraordinarily unhappy	very unhappy	unhappy	somewhat unhappy	neutral	somewhat happy	happy	very happy	extraordinarily happy
a. your present job	1	2	3	4	5	6	7	8	9
b. your organization (company)	1	2	3	4	5	6	7	8	9
c. your career progress	1	2	3	4	5	6	7	8	9
d. your family	1	2	3	4	5	6	7	8	9
e. your lifestyle	1	2	3	4	5	6	7	8	9
f. your life in general	1	2	3	4	5	6	7	8	9

- How much tension or stress is there currently in your life (circle one)?

1	2	3	4	5
none		some		a great deal

- How do you feel physically (circle one)?

1	2	3	4	5
poor	fair	good	very good	excellent

Appendix D _____

Résumés for the General Managers

Gerald Allen

Current Position

Vice President in charge of retail operations (30 branches) for New York Bank.

Career History:

- New York Bank—2 years—Trainee
- New York Bank—5 years—Branch Manager
- New York Bank—4 years—Loan Administrator for the Retail Division
- New York Bank—3 years—VP in charge of all branch offices in the Retail Division

Background:

- Born in Connecticut in 1942, first of two children
- Raised in Connecticut
- Father was a lawyer
- Received a BA from the State University of New York
- Received an MBA from University of Connecticut

Family Situation:

- Married in 1967, divorced
- Engaged again at time of study
- Two children

Bob Anderson

Current Position:

President of Ballanger Newspapers, a group of suburban newspapers owned by the Los Angeles Tribune (which in turn was owned by Magnet Communications, Inc.)

Career History:

- The Freeport News—3 years—Ad salesman and sales manager
- Graduate school—2 years
- Johnson Publishing—2 years—Business manager for two small papers
- Johnson Publishing—5 years—General manager for five small papers and a commercial printing operation
- The LA Tribune—2 years—Publisher of Ballanger Newspapers
- The LA Tribune—5 years—President of Ballanger Newspapers

Background:

- Born in Seattle in 1937, first of three children
- Raised in Seattle, mostly by his mother, who worked in TV and publishing
- Received BS from Jackson University (in Washington)
- Received MBA from the University of Washington

Family Situation:

- Married in 1961
- Two children

John Cohen

Current Position:

Chairman and CEO of Federal Specialty Stores, a national chain of specialty stores owned by American Department Stores.

Career History:

- Holly Crothers, Inc. (specialty retailing)—1 year—Trainee
- Benningtons (specialty retailing)—½ year—Trainee
- Federal—4 years—Buyer
- Federal—4 years—Merchandise Manager
- Federal—3 years—Store Manager
- Federal—3 years—President
- Federal—½ year—Chairman and CEO

Background:

- Born in California in 1939, the second of three children
- Raised in California
- Father was a manager in a specialty store
- Received BA from Princeton
- Served briefly in the Army

Family Situation:

- Married in 1963, divorced in 1966
- Remarried in 1969
- Two children

Dan Donahue

Current Position:

President of the Jordale Division of Finest Products, a large consumer products company.

Career History:

- Finest Products—1½ years—Management Training Program (NY)
- Finest Products—1 year—District Sales Manager (Ohio)
- Finest Products—3½ years—Branch Manager (NY)
- Finest Products—1½ years—International Marketing Coordinator
- Finest Products—2 years—Marketing Director in Paris
- Finest Products—2 years—VP Marketing/International (NY)
- Finest Products—2 years—GM of Europe for the paper products division
- Finest Products—1 year—Assistant to the President
- Finest Products—½ year—VP Marketing for Jordale Division
- Finest Products—2 years—President of Jordale Division

Background:

- Born in Vermont in 1937, the first of three children
- Raised in New Hampshire by relatives after parents died
- Received BS from University of New Hampshire
- Received MBA from Columbia University

Family Situation:

- Married in 1959
- Three children

Frank Firono

Current Position:

President of Tenington's, a chain of department stores located in the Southwest and owned by American Department Stores.

Career History:

- Kranston's (department store)—2 years—Trainee/Asst. Buyer
- Kranston's—2 years—Buyer
- Peterson's (department store)—1 year—Buyer
- Peterson's—2 years—Store Manager
- Peterson's—2 years—Divisional Merchandising Manager
- Peterson's—1 year—VP and General Merchandising Manager
- American Department Stores—1½ years—Executive VP for the Fable Division
- American Department Stores—1½ years—President of the Fable Division
- American Department Stores—1½ years—President and CEO of Tenington

Background:

- Born in Georgia in 1942, the third of four children
- Raised in Georgia
- Father was a veterinarian
- Received BS from Georgia State
- Received MBA from Georgia Tech

Family Situation:

- Married in 1965
- Four children

Terry Franklin

Current Position:

President and General Manager of Exeter Machine Tools, a small machine tool manufacturer owned by a European conglomerate.

Career History:

- Franklin Export—1 year—Owner/Manager/Sales
- Hellar Chemical—4 years—Sales
- Exeter Machine Tools—3 years—Sales
- Exeter Machine Tools—3 years—Sales Manager
- Exeter Machine Tools—12 years—General Manager

Background:

- Born in New Hampshire in 1924, the second of two children
- Raised in New Hampshire and New York
- Father was a sales manager
- Received BS from Rutgers
- Served in Army for three years

Family Situation:

- Married in 1945
- Four children

Chuck Gaines

Current Position:

President of the Midland Division, one of three major divisions of
Index Industries, a large midwestern manufacturer. Responsible for
revenues in the billions of dollars.

Career History:

- Index Industries—2 years—Sales Trainee in New York
- Index Industries—6 years—Sales in Columbia
- Index Industries—4 years—Sales Manager in Brazil
- Index Industries—1 year—Sales Manager in Japan
- Index Industries—4 years—Managing Director in Japan
- Index Industries—3 years—VP Index International
- Index Industries—1½ years—Assistant to Corporate President
- Index Industries—1½ years—President of Firebrand, a U.S. sub-
  sidiary of Index
- Index Industries—1 year—President of the Midland Division

Background:

- Born in New York in 1930, the last of three children
- Raised outside of U.S.
- Father in sales
- Received BA at a small college in Connecticut
- Served in the Coast Guard

Family Situation:

- Married in 1950
- Two children

Paul Jackson

Current Position:

Vice Chairman of Index Industries, a large midwestern manufacturer. In charge of the Diversified Products Division, which has over $1 billion in sales.

Career History:

- Index Industries—4 years—Training program
- U.S. Navy—3 years
- Index Industries—2 years—Production supervisor
- Index Industries—7 years—Plant manager
- Index Industries—2 years—Corporate Engineering Manager
- Index Industries—20 years—Head of Diversified Products Division (title went from Vice President to Executive Vice President to Vice Chairman)

Background:

- Born in Owens, Nebraska, in 1919, the second of three children
- Raised in Wyoming and Montana
- Father was a farmer (agribusiness)
- Received BS from University of Nebraska
- Served three years in the Navy

Family Situation:

- Married in 1944
- Remarried after death of first wife (1968) in 1973
- Three children (first marriage)

Tom Long

Current Position

Eastern region general manager for International Computers. In charge of 20 sales/service offices.

Career History:

- Fairchild Life Insurance—2 years—Trainee and supervisor in underwriting department
- Phillips Manufacturing—1 year—Sales
- International Computers—1 year—Assistant sales representative
- International Computers—½ year—Sales Representative
- International Computers—1 year—Account Representative
- International Computers—1 year—Sales Program Manager
- International Computers—1 year—Area Sales Manager
- International Computers—1 year—Sales Planning Coordinator at headquarters
- International Computers—½ year—Special Assignment (assistant to branch manager)
- International Computers—1 year—Branch Manager (different location)
- International Computers—2 years—Branch Operations Manager (in a regional office)
- International Computers—1 year—National Service Operations Manager (at corporate)
- International Computers—1 year—Eastern Regional General Manager

Background:

- Born in Indiana in 1942, the second of three children
- Raised in Virginia and Florida
- Received BS from the University of Florida
- Did some graduate work for an MBA

Family Situation:

- Married in 1962. Divorced
- Remarried in 1970
- Five children

Jack Martin

Current Position:

President and publisher of *World News,* one of a number of magazines owned by the Garland Corporation (which in turn was owned by Magnet Communications, Inc.)

Career History:

- Landry Specialty Stores—½ year—Clerk at store
- The Garland Corporation—3 years—Circulation representative
- The Garland Corporation—1 year—Training program
- The Garland Corporation—3 years—Advertising Sales
- The Garland Corporation—3 years—Advertising sales at corporate headquarters
- J. W. Thomas Advertising—1 year—Account executive
- Zalor (Ad Agency)—2 years—Account executive
- The Garland Corporation—2 years—Advertising Sales
- The Garland Corporation—9 years—Ad/sales management
- The Garland Corporation—1 year—Ad/sales management for a different publication
- The Garland Corporation—5 years—President and publisher of *World News*

Background:

- Born in Michigan in 1926, the first of two children
- Raised in Michigan
- Father was an engineer and salesman
- Received BA from the University of Michigan
- Served in the Marines for three years

Family Situation:

- Married in 1950
- Five children

Richard Papolis

Current Position:

President of the Datatrack Division of International Computers, Inc.

Career History:

- Johnson Research—3 years—Engineer
- DLC, Inc.—5 years—Assistant Technical Director
- Fairfield Lewis—5 years—Technical Director
- Fairfield Lewis—8 years—Division Manager
- Datatrack (helped start company)—7 years—President
- International Computers (they bought Datatrack)—4 years—
- President and head of the Datatrack Division

Background:

- Born in Greece in 1927, the fourth of four children
- Raised in Greece
- Father was a sea captain
- Received BS from UCLA
- Received MS from UCLA

Family Situation:

- Married in 1952, later divorced
- Remarried in 1971
- Two children

Richard Poullin

Current Position:

President of the television division of Magnet Communications, Inc.

Career History:

- Magnet Communications—5 years—Corporate Financial Analyst
- Magnet Communications—3 years—Assistant to the Chairman of Magnet
- Magnet Communications—2 years—Assistant to the Financial VP of Magnet (responsibility for the television and film division)
- Magnet Communications—½ year—Assistant to the Group VP overseeing television and film division
- Magnet Communications—3 years—General Manager of film division
- Magnet Communications—2 years—President of the television division

Background:

- Born in Massachusetts in 1940, first of four children
- Raised in seven different cities in the US and elsewhere
- Father was a career Air Force Officer
- Received BS from Harvard
- Received MBA from Wharton

Family Situation:

- Married in 1963, divorced in 1969
- Remarried in 1973
- One child

Michael Richardson

Current Position:

President and CEO of Lipton-Johnson, an Eastern investment management company.

Career History:

- Pennings, Inc. (investment management)—2 years—Investment Analyst
- Lipton-Johnson (helped start this company)—1 year—Investment Analyst
- Lipton-Johnson—5 years—Portfolio manager
- Lipton-Johnson—9 years—VP Marketing
- Lipton-Johnson—5 years—President and CEO

Background:

- Born in Hartford, Conn., in 1934, the fourth of six children
- Raised near Boston
- Father was a manufacturing executive
- Received BA from Harvard
- Received MBA from Wharton

Family Situation:

- Married in 1962
- Two children

B. J. Sparksman

Current Position:

Managing partner of the Houston office of Benson and Co., a very large professional services company.

Career History:

- Thomas Oil—2 years—Accountant/assistant manager
- Egis Chemical—2 years—Treasury staff
- Rollins Oil Transport—1 year—Controller
- FLD Food Stores—1 year—Controller
- FLD Food Stores—2 years—Financial VP
- Benson and Company—5 years—Consultant
- Benson and Company—2 years—Partner
- Benson and Company—4 years—Partner in charge of one business area in Fort Worth
- Benson and Company—3 years—Partner in charge of the same business area in Houston
- Benson and Company—1 year—Managing Partner in Houston

Background:

- Born in Lupton, Alabama, in 1929, the fourth of five children
- Raised in Alabama
- Father was a mail carrier
- Received BA from the University of Alabama
- Received an MBA from SMU
- Served four years in the Air Force

Family Situation

- Married in 1951
- One child

John Thompson

Current Position:

> Senior Vice President and head of the Commercial Finance Division of New York Bank.

Career History:

- Nitro Steel—3 years—Credit manager
- Nitro Steel—3 years—Credit manager (different city)
- Nitro Steel—3 years—Regional Credit Manager
- New York Bank—5 years—Lending Officer in the Commercial Finance Division
- New York Bank—10 years—Manager of one of the businesses in Commercial Finance
- New York Bank—½ year—Head of Commercial Finance

Background:

- Born in Ohio in 1931, the second of two children
- Raised in Ohio
- Father was in banking
- Received BS from the University of Cincinnati
- Served two years in the US Army

Family Situation:

- Married in 1963
- Two children

Appendix E _____

Appraising GM Performance

BECAUSE OF THE VERY NATURE of GM jobs, it is somewhat difficult to assess how effective an incumbent is or to rank the effectiveness of different GMs. This is so for two major reasons. First, some aspects of a GM's responsibilities are difficult to measure precisely. In particular, how well a GM handles his longer-run responsibilities is often very difficult to measure in the short run. Second, no single formula exists to weigh performance in different areas. Managers and academics could argue endlessly over whether meeting profit objectives, for example, should count for 20 or 50 or 80 percent of the overall appraisal.

In this study, rating performance is made even more difficult by the relatively narrow performance range. As noted before, all of the GMs were doing at least a fair-to-good job; no one was obviously failing. A wider range would make it easier to distinguish various levels of performance.

The Method Employed

Nevertheless, despite these difficulties, it was possible to appraise the performance of our GMs roughly by using the following strategy:

1. I did not try to distinguish more than three levels of performance: good/fair, very good, and excellent.
2. If the GM had been in the job a relatively short time (less than one year), I did not even try to rate his performance.

3. We used both "hard" and "soft" measures. The hard measures included sales, profit, and other financial indices. The soft measures included peer, subordinate, and boss judgments as well as, when possible, judgements from informed sources in the investment community.

The Rating

Using this procedure, our fifteen general managers fell into the following categories:

1. Excellent. Two of the GMs seem clearly to belong in this category; they are Richard Papolis and Richard Poullin. Bottom line measures of their performance (net income) consistently grew at a high rate (greater than 30 percent per year), never falling below objectives. Their subordinates, peers, and bosses generally agreed that they were doing an excellent job. Only two people in one case, and three in the other, rated their performance as less than excellent. The two people from the investment community with whom I spoke agreed with the majority of others; they felt Papolis and Poullin were doing an outstanding job.
2. Very good. Six of the GMs fall into this category: Bob Anderson, Dan Donahue, Frank Firono, Tom Long, Jack Martin, and Michael Richardson. Each was producing very good bottom-line results, although not nearly as spectacular as those of the two GMs in the first group. Opinions from subordinates, peers, bosses, and outside analysts regarding their performances ranged from good to excellent.
3. Good/Fair. Three GMs fall into this category; they are Gerald Allen, Terry Franklin, and Paul Jackson. These men did not always achieve their bottom-line objectives. Their businesses tended to be growing less than others and were less profitable. The opinions of others ranged from poor to excellent, with most people saying that the GMs were doing a "good job" or a "pretty good job."
4. Unclear. Four GMs fall here, all because they had not been in their jobs long enough to be judged fairly. This category includes John Cohen, Chuck Gaines. B. J. Sparksman, and John Thompson.

Notes _____

Chapter 1

1. (Cambridge, Mass.: Harvard University Press, 1977), p. 4.
2. An enormous amount of literature exists regarding the subject of "management." However, most of this literature concerns management processes in organizations or managerial tools, not who managers are, what they do, or why some are more effective and successful than others. For example, chapters from a typical textbook on management (Trewartha and Newport's *Management;* Dallas: Business Publications, 1976) include "Operational Decision-Making Systems," "Marketing and Production Controls," "Communication and Information Systems." This book has no chapter or set of chapters on "managerial behavior," or "managerial jobs," or "managers." The literature which does focus on managers is mostly prescriptive. That is, it is someone's advice based on generalized experience or on deduction from a theory. At its best, this writing is thought-provoking and insightful. The bulk of this literature, however, is of questionable value. For an excellent discussion of this issue see John P. Campbell, Marvin D. Dunnette, Edward F. Lawler, III, and Karl Weick, Jr., *Managerial Behavior, Performance, and Effectiveness* (Englewood Cliffs, N.J.: Prentice-Hall, 1970), especially page 6.
3. Indeed, much of the most interesting work on managers to date

has come in the form of general observations and insights from very perceptive individuals or from single case studies, not from systematic studies of the type reported here. Such individuals include Peter Drucker (see *Management* [New York: Harper and Row, 1974], and *The Effective Executive* [New York: Harper and Row, 1967]), Chester Barnard (*The Functions of the Executive* [Cambridge, Mass.: Harvard University Press, 1939]), Abe Zaleznik (*The Human Dilemma of Leadership* [New York: Harper and Row, 1966]), and Doug McGregor (*The Professional Manager* [New York: Mc-Graw-Hill, 1967]). The kind of case studies to which I am referring can be found in *Policy Formulation and Administration* by Christensen, Berg, and Salter (Homewood, Ill.: Irwin, 1976), and in *Business Policy* by Christensen, Andrews, and Bower (Homewood, Ill.: Irwin, 1978).

4. *Executive Behavior* (Stockholm: Stromberg Aktiebulag, 1951).

5. *The Nature of Managerial Work* (New York: Harper and Row, 1973).

6. In "Leadership: Beyond Establishment Views," from a presentation at the Sixth Biennial Leadership Symposium at Southern Illinois University at Carbondale, October, 1980, p. 19.

7. Some people use the term general manager to refer only to a CEO or a president of a firm. We employ a broader definition here, but one that is not uncommon.

8. To my knowledge, no one has ever before systematically studied so many high-level executives in this much depth. For example, in his ground-breaking study, Mintzberg focused on fewer people (five) and relied almost entirely on observation. Another well-known study (*The Gamesman* [New York: Simon and Schuster, 1976]) by Michael Maccoby focused mostly on lower-level managers and relied only on relatively short, one-shot interviews.

9. Such a small number obviously cannot yield conclusive proof of any hypothesis. Then again, proving theories was not the purpose of this investigation. The chief objective was to generate tentative answers and generalizations about important issues. The methodological philosophy employed here is consistent with a tradition of work which seeks to focus in a holistic, dynamic, and exploratory way on some phenomena. For an excellent example of recent work guided by this philosophy, see *The Seasons of a Man's Life* by Dan Levenson et al.(New York: Alfred A. Knopf, 1978).

10. All names have been disguised.

11. See "The Profession of Management" in *The New Republic*, July 27, 1981.

12. This is consistent with what others have found. For example, C. L.

Shartle quotes a marvelous piece of dialogue in his book *Executive Performance and Leadership* (Englewood Cliffs, N.J.: Prentice-Hall, 1956), p. 82, in which a researcher tries to get an executive to tell him what he does.

13. Instead of a literature review at this point, relevant literature will be footnoted in the data-presentation chapters. This approach has been chosen for a number of reasons. First, because the book is written for both managerial and academic audiences, every effort has been made to include in the text only those subjects of interest to both groups. Issues of interest to only an academic audience have been put in footnotes and appendices. Second, because of the state of the literature on executive work and behavior, a literature review would tend to be extremely short (if it included only comparable studies or real theories of executive behavior) or extremely long (if it included all the work in management and the applied social sciences that is in some way relevant). The former isn't very useful, and the latter isn't very practical. Finally, I agree with Mintzberg that we know very little in this area (though perhaps more than "1%"). I have found that, when little good empirical or theoretical work exists in an area, literature reviews can distract more than help.

Chapter 2

1. This way of conceptualizing managerial jobs has roots both in managerial practice (see, for example, Max Wortman and JoAnn Sperling, *Defining the Manager's Job*, [New York: AMACOM, 1975]) and in the literature (see Robert J. DeFillippi and Robert H. Miles, "Core Typology of Managerial Role Behavior" [unpublished article], 1979).

2. See, for example, the conclusions reached by Henry Mintzberg, Duru Raisingani, and Andre Theoret in "The Structure of Unstructured Decision Process," *ASQ* (June 1976), pp. 250–251, and *Business Policy* by C. Roland Christensen, Ken Andrews, and Joe Bower (Homewood, Ill.: Richard A. Irwin, 1978).

3. See, for example, "General Managers in the Middle" by Hugo Uyterhoeven, *Harvard Business Review* (March/April, 1972) and Joseph L. Bower, *Managing the Resource Allocation Process* (Boston, Mass.: HBS Division of Research, 1970).

4. See Henry Mintzberg, *The Nature of Managerial Work* (New York: Harper and Row, 1973).

5. See, for example, Wick Skinner and W. Earl Sasser, "Managers with

Impact: Versatile and Inconsistent," *HBR* (November/December 1977); John Gabarro and John Kotter, "Managing Your Boss," *HBR* (January/February 1980); and Rosemary Stewart, "To Understand the Manager's Job: Consider Demands, Constraints, Choices," *Organizational Dynamics* (Spring, 1976).

6. See Hugo Uyterhoeven, "General Managers in the Middle," *Harvard Business Review* (March/April 1977).

7. See Leonard Sayles, *Managerial Behavior* (New York: McGraw-Hill, 1964).

8. See Abraham Zaleznik, *The Human Dilemma of Leadership,* (New York: Harper and Row, 1967); Hugo Uyterhoeven, "General Managers in the Middle," *Harvard Business Review* (March/April, 1972); Wickham Skinner and W. Earl Sasser, "Managers with Impact: Versatile and Inconsistent," *Harvard Business Review* (November/December, 1977).

9. Indirectly, of course, still other factors can create differences by modifying the job, the business, or the corporation. The most obvious of these factors is the GM himself and the length of time he has been in his job. As such, these jobs are not static; they are alive and evolve over time. More on this in Chapters 4 and 5.

10. See Alfred Chandler, Jr., *Strategy and Structure* (Cambridge, Mass.: MIT Press, 1962), and Joseph L. Bower, *Managing the Resource Allocation Process* (Boston, Mass.: HBS Division of Research, 1970) for early documentation of this trend.

11. Group GMs tend to be found in only fairly large companies. Yet in July, 1979, 30 percent of the Fortune 500 companies had no group GMs. See Allen F. Juers, "The Group Executive," *Management Review* (March 1979).

12. The key exception has been the work of Rosemary Stewart.

13. See Stewart's work; J. Child and T. Ellis, "Predictors of Variations in Managerial Roles," *Human Relations 26,* 2 (1973): 227–250; H. Stieglitz, "The Chief Executive's Job and the Size of the Company," *The Conference Board Record* (September 1970); J. Bower, *Managing The Resource Allocation Process* (Cambridge, Mass.: Harvard Business School, 1970); and B. Scott, "Stages of Corporate Development" (Boston, Mass.: Intercollegiate Case Clearing House, 1971).

14. For example, see Paul Lawrence and Jay Lorsch, *Organization and Environment,* (Cambridge, Mass.: Harvard Business School, 1967); James Thompson, *Organizations in Action,* (Englewood Cliffs, N.J.: Prentice-Hall, 1967); Peter Blau, *On the Nature of Organizations,* (New York: Wiley, 1974); and a recent study by Peter Grinyer and

Masoud Yasi-Ardekani, "Strategy, Structure, Size, and Bureaucracy," *Academy of Management Journal 24*, 3 (1981).

Chapter 3

1. Because of limitations participants placed on the amount of time they could devote to personal interviews or questionnaires, only one standard instrument was used (the Strong-Campbell). Hence, most of the data that supports these themes come from interviews with people who knew the GMs (about ten people per site). This was supplemented with data from observation, interviews with the GMs, and the Strong-Campbell.

2. Those whose performance was rated "excellent" (see Appendix E for the method) expressed a job satisfaction averaging 8.5 (on a 1–9 scale). Those whose performance was rated "very good" expressed a job satisfaction of 8.1. Those with a performance rated at good/fair put their job satisfaction at 6.0.

3. Those GMs who were making considerably more money than others their age expressed a career satisfaction of 8.7 (on a 1–9 scale). Those who were making about the same as others their age expressed a satisfaction with their careers of 7.7. Those making less money than others their age averaged only 7.2.

4. The two most obvious exceptions to this pattern were the two entrepreneurs in the study.

5. Specifically, they scored over 40 on one or more scales associated with all of the basic business functions (see Appendix C for information about the Strong-Campbell). These functions and the associated scales are:

   - Finance: banker, investment fund manager, accountant, credit manager
   - Marketing/sales: computer sales, life insurance agent, sales manager, buyer, department store sales, advertising executive, realtor
   - Operations: army officer, navy officer, purchasing agent, department store manager, merchant marine officer
   - Personnel: personnel director
   - Legal: lawyer
   - External/government relations: chamber of commerce executive, public administrator

6. This type of pattern, based on my own experience with the Strong-Campbell, is rarely found in the responses of people taking this test.

7. If this sounds far-fetched, recall that scientists currently estimate that one human brain can store nearly ten times as much information as is in the National Archives, or the equivalent of 400,000 sets of the *Encyclopaedia Britannica* (RCA Corporation's Advanced Technological Laboratories' estimate).

8. See, for example, Thomas Harrell, *Managers' Performance and Personality* (Dallas: Southwest Publishing, 1961), chap. 10; Ed Schein, "The General Manager: A profile," Distinguished Management Scholar lecture given at the Eastern Academy of Management, May 5, 1972; and David McClelland, *Power: The Inner Experience,* New York: Irvington, 1975), chap. 7. For a general review of literature on the personal characteristics of managers, see John Campbell, Marvin Dunnette, Edward Lawler, III, and Karl Weick, Jr., *Managerial Behavior, Performance, and Effectiveness* (New York: McGraw-Hill, 1970).

9. As Ed Schein has pointed out before, one of the key problems in locating effective general managers may be that this diverse set of characteristics exists in only a limited number of people. See *Organizational Psychology,* Third Edition (Englewood Cliffs, N.J.: Prentice-Hall, 1980), pp. 131–132.

10. Regarding the levels of success they had achieved: The average income (1978) of the two excellent performers, whose ages averaged 46, was $160,000. The average income of the six very good performers, whose average age was 44, was $126,000. The income of the three good/fair performers, average age 51, was $125,000.

11. See *Fortune* (May 1976), pp. 176–177.

12. See *Management Review* (July 1979), pp. 15–20.

13. See *The Chief Executive and His Job,* Studies in Personnel Policy, No. 214 (1969).

14. See "The Chief Executive: Background and Attitude Profiles," a report by Arthur Young, the accounting firm (1980).

15. See George Farris, "Executive Cohesiveness and Financial Performance of the Fortune 500," delivered at the 1979 Management Meeting in Atlanta.

16. See Harrell, *Managers' Performance and Personality,* for additional confirmation of a variety of background characteristics. For further evidence of the "success syndrome," see Tim Hall, *Careers in Organization* (Santa Monica, Cal.: Goodyear, 1976). This is also consistent with recent empirical research by Rosenbaum. See "Tournament Mobility: Career Patterns in a Corporation," *Administrative Science Quarterly* (June 1979).

17. See "How Chief Executives Get to the Top," *Chief Executive* (December 1980).

18. For example, see Robert W. White, *Lives in Progress* (New York: Holt, Rinehart and Winston, 1966).

19. See *Business Week* (February 25, 1980), p. 166.

20. The most notable general exception is Rosemary Stewart. See, for example, *Managers and Their Jobs* (New York: Macmillan, 1967); *Contrasts in Management* (New York: McGraw-Hill, 1976); and *The District Administration for the National Health Service* (London: King's Fund, 1980). One recent more specific exception is James Hall, "Organizational Technology and Executive Successes," *California Management Review* (Fall 1976).

21. In general, from the background questionnaire given to the GMs, it appears that the following are all related: (1) high stress; (2) very high level of career success to date [rapid movement]; (3) long work hours; (4) in current job less than one year [still getting up to speed]; (5) relatively low satisfaction with family and lifestyle.

22. A good example appeared recently in *The Wall Street Journal;* see "Migrant Managers: A New Road to the Top," July 17, 1980.

23. An excellent exception by Bob Hayes and Bill Abernathy is "Managing Our Way to Economic Decline," *Harvard Business Review* (July/August 1980).

Chapter 4

1. Kenneth Andrews, *The Concept of Corporate Strategy* (Homewood, Ill.: Dow Jones-Irwin, 1971), p. 18.

2. In previous work (see *Organizational Dynamics*), I have found it useful when speaking of the behavior of a system to distinguish between behaviors in different time frames (a day, a month, a year, ten years, etc.). I have found that different concepts and different relationships tend to be important depending upon the time frame. This finding seems to be appropriate here also, and provides the basis for the organization of this chapter.

3. See, for example, J. B. Quinn, *Strategies for Change; Logical Incrementalism* (Homewood, Ill.: Richard D. Irwin, 1980); Henry Mintzberg, *The Nature of Managerial Work* (New York: Harper and Row, 1973); H. Edward Wrapp, "Good Managers Don't Make Policy Decisions," *Harvard Business Review* (September/October 1967); Charles Lindblom, "The Science of 'Muddling Through'," *Public Administration Review 19* (1959), pp. 79–88; James March and Herbert Simon,

Organizations (New York: John Wiley, 1958); Chester Barnard, *The Functions of the Executive* (Cambridge, Mass.: Harvard University Press, 1939); Rosemary Stewart, "Managerial Agendas—Reactive or Proactive," *Organizational Dynamics* (Autumn 1979); Frank Aguilar, *Scanning the Business Environment* (New York: Macmillan, 1967); and Michael McCaskey, "A Contingency Approach to Planning: Planning with Goals and Planning without Goals," *Academy of Management Journal* (June, 1974).

4. See, for example, Jack Gabarro, "Socialization at the Top—How CEOs and their Subordinates Evolve Interpersonal Contacts," *Organizational Dynamics* (Winter 1979); Jeff Pfeffer and Jerry Salancik, "Who Gets Power and How They Hold on to It," *Organizational Dynamics* (Winter 1977); John Kotter, "Power, Dependence, and Effective Management," *Harvard Business Review* (July/August 1977); Melville Nalton, *Men Who Manage* (New York: Wiley, 1959); and Richard Pascale and Tony Athos, *The Art of Japanese Management* (New York: Simon and Schuster, 1981).

5. A more detailed discussion of this can be found in my book, *Power in Management* (New York: AMACOM, 1979), chap. 4.

6. See recent work by Tom Peters and Jeff Pfeffer in particular; for example, Peters, "Symbols, Patterns, and Settings: An Optimistic Case for Getting Things Done," *Organizational Dynamics* 7 (1978); and Pfeffer, "Management as Symbolic Action," *Research in Organizational Behavior 3*, ed. Larry Cummings and Barry Staw (Greenwich, Conn.: JAI Press, 1980). Also see Andrew M. Pettigrew, *The Politics of Organizational Decision Making* (London: Tavistock Publications, Ltd., 1973) and John Kotter, "Power, Dependence and Effective Management," *Harvard Business Review* (July/August 1977).

7. I am thinking particularly about conclusions regarding how much information the mind can process and about how much of this is done intuitively. See John D. Steinbruner, *The Cybernetic Theory of Decision* (Princeton, N.J.: Princeton University Press, 1974), p. 92.

8. Such as Sune Carlson, *Executive Behavior: A Study of the Work Load and the Working Methods of Managing Directors* (Stockholm: Strombergs, 1951); T. Burns, "Management in Action," *Operational Research Quarterly 8* (1957); Rosemary Stewart, "To Understand the Manager's Job: Consider Demands, Constraints, Choices," *Organizational Dynamics* (1957); Michael Cohen and James March, *Leadership and Ambiguity* (New York: McGraw-Hill, 1974); R. Dubin and S. L. Spray, "Executive Behavior and Interaction," *Industrial Relations 3* (1964): 99–108; E. Brewer and J. W. C. Tomlinson, "The Manager's Working Day," *The Journal of Industrial Economics 12* (1964): 191–197.

9. See Morgan McCall, Ann Morrison, and Robert Hannan, "Studies of Managerial Work: Results and Methods," Technical Report No. 9 (Greensboro, N.C.: Center for Creative Leadership, 1978). This excellent report summarizes dozens of different studies ranging from S. Carson's groundbreaking work in 1951 to recent work by Mintzberg, Stewart, and others.

10. See *The Nature of Managerial Work* (New York: Harper and Row, 1973).

11. "Leadership: Sad Facts and Silver Linings," *Harvard Business Review* (November/December 1979).

Chapter 6

1. There are limits to what can be said here because this was not a study of corporate- or university-based efforts to improve the effectiveness of general managers. Nevertheless, here are many clues regarding which managerial practices inhibit or promote excellent performance and how formal education and research can contribute in this regard. Of necessity, much of the discussion in this chapter will be more speculative than that in the rest of the book, but it is speculation on issues of great importance to managers and management educators alike.

2. From *The New Republic,* June 27, 1981, p. 27.

3. See, for example, Herbert Meyer, "The Headhunters Come Upon Golden Days," *Fortune* (October 8, 1978), p. 110.

4. The only study of which I am aware that speaks directly to this point reaches the same conclusions. See Y. K. Shetty and N. S. Perry, Jr., "Are Top Executives Transferable Across Companies?" *Business Horizons* (June 1976).

5. See "More Companies Look within for Managers," *Wall Street Journal,* October 28, 1980, p. 37.

6. For example, see the recent *Wall Street Journal* article, "Some Companies Try to Spot Leaders Early, Guide Them to the Top," February 25, 1981.

7. See, for example, "Wanted: A Manager to Fit Each Strategy," *Business Week* (February 25, 1980), pp. 166–173.

8. See Rumelt's *Strategy, Structure, and Economic Performance* (Boston, Mass.: Harvard Business School, 1974) for a study comparing performance by conglomerates to other kinds of corporations.

9. Tom Peters has found that some high-performing corporations do

just this. See "Putting Excellence into Management," *Business Week,* July 21, 1980, pp. 196–197.

10. The lack of public information regarding how young and older executives are different fuels this problem, as do studies which suggest there are no differences. For example, a recent article in *Esquire* magazine suggests that despite the rise in the divorce rate among the population at large, those at the top in business are "still wed to wife number 1." See "No Divorce at the Top," *Esquire,* June 19, 1979, page 8.

11. See, for example, Thomas W. Harrell, *Manager's Performance and Personality* (Dallas: Southwest Publishing Co., 1961).

12. For example, with respect to intuition, see Henry Mintzberg, "Planning on the Left Side and Managing on the Right," *Harvard Business Review* (July/August 1976); Roy Rowan, "Hunches Are More than Blind Faith," *Fortune* (April 23, 1979); and Mike McCaskey, *Managing Ambiguity* (Marshfield, Mass.: Pitman, 1982).

13. See *Self Assessment and Career Development* (Englewood Cliffs, N.J.: Prentice-Hall, 1978).

14. See, for example, the review of this work in Thomas W. Harrell, *Manager's Performance and Personality* (Dallas: Southwest Publishing Company, 1961).

15. See the discussion of this point in Campbell et al., *Managerial Behavior, Performance and Effectiveness* (Englewood Cliffs, N.J.: Prentice-Hall, 1970).

16. Ibid.

17. See Ralph Stogdill, *Handbook of Leadership* (New York: Free Press, 1974), and James Tolliver and Orlando Behling, "Leadership Theory: Some Implications for Managers," *MSU Business Topics,* Summer 1978.

18. See Chapter 13 in Campbell et al.

19. See Morgan McCall and Michael Lombardo, *Leadership: Where Else Can We Go?* (Durham, N.C.: Duke University Press, 1978).

20. See Fritz Roethlisberger and William Dickson, *Management and the Worker* (Cambridge, Mass.: Harvard University Press, 1939); Henry Mintzberg, *The Nature of Managerial Work,* (New York: Harper and Row, 1973); and Joseph L. Bower, *Managing the Resource Allocation Process* (Boston: HBS Division of Research, 1970).

21. On p. 312 of *Street Corner Society,* Whyte gives a perfect example of this.

22. Ibid., p. 293.

23. Ibid., p. 300.

24. Ibid., p. 303.
25. See ibid., p. 302, for example.
26. Ibid., p. 301.
27. Ibid., p. 322.
28. Ibid., p. 311.

Appendix A

1. The works which I believe influenced me most include Henry Mintzberg, *The Nature of Managerial Work* (New York: Harper and Row, 1973); Rosemary Stewart, *Managers and Their Jobs* (New York: Macmillan, 1967); Leonard Sayles, *Managerial Behavior,* and J. P. Campbell et al., *Managerial Behavior, Performance and Effectiveness* (Englewood Cliffs, N.J.: Prentice-Hall, 1970).

2. Most of my other work has been reported in five books: *Mayors in Action,* with Paul Lawrence (New York: Wiley, 1974); *Self Assessment and Career Development,* with Victor Faux and Charles McArthur (Englewood Cliffs, N.J.: Prentice-Hall, 1978); *Organizational Dynamics* (Reading, Mass.: Addison-Wesley, 1978); *Organization,* with Len Schlesinger and Vijay Sathe (Homewood, Ill.: Irwin, 1979); and *Power in Management* (New York: AMACOM, 1979).

3. In an excellent report entitled *Studies of Managerial Work* (Technical Report 9, Center for Creative Leadership, May 1978), McCall, Morrison, and Hannan argue for just this type of design. They conclude (p. 44) that "if managerial behavior is of interest, it is clear that questionnaires are not a good way to get at it. . . . Rather, multiple-method research designs are needed to reconcile how general-management responsibilities (such as planning) play out within the chaotic activity patterns in a manager's daily life."

4. One GM was promoted before I could make the final visit. In one other setting, I was not able to interview the GM's boss.

Appendix C

1. One of the consequences of setting the occupational group's score at 50 is that it is possible to get a negative score on many of the scales.

2. For previous versions of this instrument, Strong verified the predictive values of the occupational scales for eighteen years after the test was taken (E. K. Strong, Jr., *Vocational Interests 18 Years after College,* (Minneapolis: University of Minnesota Press, 1955); McArthur

showed they predicted for fourteen years (McArthur, "Long-Term Validity of the Strong Vocational Interest in Two Subcultures," *Journal of Applied Psychology* [1954], pp. 346–533). These and other research efforts have found that the odds that the following statements will turn out to be true range from 2 to 1 up to 5 to 1 with 3.5 being the commonest result.

a. People continuing in occupation X obtained a higher interest score in X than in any other occupation.

b. People continuing in occupation X obtained a higher interest score in X than other people entering other occupations.

c. People continuing in occupation X obtained higher scores in X than people who change from X to another occupation.

d. People changing from occupation X to occupation Y scored higher in Y prior to the change than in any other occupation, including X.

Bibliography

AGUILAR, FRANK. *Scanning the Business Environment.* New York: Macmillan, 1967.

ANDREWS, KENNETH. *The Concept of Corporate Strategy.* Homewood, Ill.: Dow Jones-Irwin, 1971.

BARNARD, CHESTER. *The Functions of the Executive.* Cambridge, Mass.: Harvard University Press, 1939.

BLAU, PETER. *On the Nature of Organizations.* New York: Wiley, 1974.

BOWER, JOSEPH L. *Managing the Resource Allocation Process.* Boston: HBS Division of Research, 1970.

BOYATIZIS, RICHARD. *The Competent Manager.* New York: Wiley, 1981.

BREWER, E. and J. W. C. TOMLINSON. "The Manager's Working Day," *The Journal of Industrial Economics 12* (1964), pp. 191–97.

BURCK, CHARLES. "A Group Profile of The Fortune 500 Chief Executive," *Fortune* (May 1976).

BURNS, TOM. "Management in Action," *Operational Research Quarterly 8* (1957).

Business Week. "Putting Excellence into Management" (July 21, 1980), pp. 196–197.

Business Week. "Wanted: A Manager to Fit Each Strategy" (February 25, 1980), pp. 166–173.

CAMPBELL, JOHN P., MARVIN D. DUNNETTE, EDWARD E. LAWLER III, and KARL WEICK, JR., *Managerial Behavior, Performance and Effectiveness.* Englewood Cliffs, N.J.: Prentice-Hall, 1970.

CARLSON, SUNE, *Executive Behavior: A Study of the Work Load and the Working Methods of Managing Directors.* Stockholm: Strombergs, 1951.

CHANDLER, ALFRED, JR. *Strategy and Structure.* Cambridge, Mass.: MIT Press, 1962.

CHANDLER, ALFRED, JR. *The Visible Hand.* Cambridge, Mass.: Harvard University Press, 1977.

Chief Executive. "How Chief Executives Get to the Top" (December 1980).

The Chief Executive and His Job. The Conference Board Studies in Personnel Policy, No. 214, 1969.

CHILD, JOHN and T. ELLIS. "Predictors of Variations in Managerial Roles," *Human Relations 26,* 2 (1973), pp. 227–250.

COHEN, MICHAEL and JAMES MARCH. *Leadership and Ambiguity.* New York: McGraw-Hill, 1974.

CHRISTENSEN, C. ROLAND, KEN ANDREWS, and JOE BOWER. *Business Policy.* Homewood, Ill.: Richard D. Irwin, 1978.

DALTON, MELVILLE. *Men Who Manage.* New York: Wiley, 1959.

DEFILIPPI, ROBERT J. and ROBERT H. MILES. "Core Typology of Managerial Role Behavior." Unpublished article, 1979.

DRUCKER, PETER. *The Age of Discontinuity.* New York: Harper and Row, 1969.

DRUCKER, PETER. *The Practice of Management.* New York: Harper and Row, 1954.

DUBIN, R. and S. L. SPRAY. "Executive Behavior and Interaction," *Industrial Relations 3* (1964), pp. 99–108.

FARRIS, GEORGE. "Executive Cohesiveness and Financial Performers for the Fortune 500." Delivered at the 1979 Academy of Management meeting in Atlanta.

FIEDLER, FRED E. *A Theory of Leadership Effectiveness.* New York: McGraw-Hill, 1967.

GABARRO, JACK. "Socialization at the Top—How CEOs and their Subordinates Evolve Interpersonal Contacts," *Organizational Dynamics* (Winter 1979).

GALBRAITH, JAY. *Organizational Design.* Reading, Mass.: Addison-Wesley, 1973.

GRINYER, PETER and MASOUD YASI-ARDEKANI. "Strategy, Structure, Size, and Bureaucracy," *Academy of Management Journal 3,* 1981.

HALL, JAMES. "Organizational Technology and Executive Succession," *California Management Review* (Fall 1976).

HALL, TIM. *Careers in Organizations.* Santa Monica, Calif.: Goodyear, 1976.

HARRELL, THOMAS W. *Manager's Performance and Personality.* Dallas: Southwest Publishing Co., 1961.

HAYES, BOB and BILL ABERNATHY. "Managing Our Way to Economic Decline," *Harvard Business Review* (July/August 1980).

JUERS, ALLEN F. "The Group Executive," *The Management Review* (March 1979).

KOTTER, JOHN P. and PAUL R. LAWRENCE. *Mayors in Action.* New York: Wiley, 1974.

KOTTER, JOHN P. "Power, Dependence, and Effective Management," *Harvard Business Review* (July/August 1977).

KOTTER, JOHN P. "Power, Success, and Organizational Effectiveness," *Organizational Dynamics* (Winter 1977/78).

KOTTER, JOHN P., VICTOR FAUX, and CHARLES MCARTHUR. *Self Assessment and Career Development.* Englewood Cliffs, N.J.: Prentice-Hall, 1978.

KOTTER, JOHN P. *Organizational Dynamics.* Reading, Mass.: Addison-Wesley, 1978.

KOTTER, JOHN P., LEN SCHLESINGER, and VIJAY SATHE. *Organization.* Homewood, Ill.: Irwin, 1979.

KOTTER, JOHN P. *Power in Management.* New York: AMACOM, 1979.

KOTTER, JOHN P. and JACK GABARRO. "Managing Your Boss." *Harvard Business Review* (January/February 1980).

LAWRENCE, PAUL R. and JAY LORSCH. *Organization and Environment.* Boston: Harvard Business School, 1967.

LEVINSON, DANIEL, with CHARLOTTE DARROW, EDWARD KLEIN, MARIA LEVINSON, and BRAXTON MCKEE. *The Seasons of a Man's Life.* New York: Alfred A. Knopf, 1978.

LEVINSON, HARRY. *The Exceptional Executive.* Cambridge, Mass.: Harvard University Press, 1968.

LEWIN, K., R. LIPPIT, and R. K. WHITE. "Patterns of Aggressive Behavior in Experimentally Created Social Climates," *Journal of Social Psychology 10* (1939).

LINDBLOM, CHARLES. "The Science of 'Muddling Through'," *Public Administration Review 19* (1959), pp. 79–88.

LORSCH, JAY and STEVE ALLEN. *Managing Diversity and Interdependence.* Cambridge, Mass.: Harvard University Press, 1974.

MACOBY, MICHAEL. *The Gamesman.* New York: Simon and Schuster, 1976.

MARCH, JAMES and HERBERT SIMON. *Organizations.* New York: Wiley, 1958.

McARTHUR, CHARLES. "Long Term Validity of the Strong Vocational Interest in Two Subcultures," *Journal of Applied Psychology* (1954).

McCALL, MORGAN and MICHAEL LOMBARDO. *Leadership: Where Else Can We Go?* Durham, N.C.: Duke University Press, 1978.

McCALL, MORGAN, ANN MORRISON, and ROBERT HANNAN. "Studies of Managerial Work: Results and Methods." Technical Report #9. Greensboro, N.C.: Center for Creative Leadership, May 1978.

McCASKEY, MICHAEL. "A Contingency Approach to Planning: Planning with Goals and Planning without Goals," *Academy of Management Journal* (June 1974).

McCASKEY, MICHAEL. *Managing Ambiguity.* Marshfield, Mass.: Pitman, 1982.

McCLELLAND, DAVID. *Power: The Inner Experience.* New York: Irvington, 1975.

McGREGOR, DOUGLAS. *The Human Side of Enterprise.* New York: McGraw-Hill, 1960.

McGREGOR, DOUGLAS. *The Professional Manager.* New York: McGraw-Hill, 1967.

MEYER, HERBERT. "The Headhunters Come Upon Golden Days," *Fortune* (October 8, 1978).

MINTZBERG, HENRY. *The Nature of Managerial Work.* New York: Harper and Row, 1973.

MINTZBERG, HENRY. "The Manager's Job: Folklore and Fact," *Harvard Business Review* (July/August 1975).

MINTZBERG, HENRY. "Planning on the Left Side and Management on the Right," *Harvard Business Review* (July/August 1976).

MINTZBERG, HENRY. "Leadership: Beyond Establishment Views." From a presentation at the Sixth Biennial Leadership Symposium at Southern Illinois University at Carbondale, October 1980.

MINTZBERG, HENRY, DURU RAISINGANI, and ANDRE THEORET. "The Structure of Unstructured Decision Process," *Administrative Science Quarterly* (June 1976).

PASCALE, RICHARD and TONY ATHOS. *The Art of Japanese Management.* New York: Simon and Schuster, 1981.

PETERS, TOM. "Symbols, Patterns, and Settings: An Optimistic Case for Getting Things Done," *Organizational Dynamics* (1978).

PETERS, TOM. "Leadership: Sad Facts and Silver Linings," *Harvard Business Review* (November/December 1979).

PETTIGREW, ANDREW M. *The Politics of Organizational Decision-Making.* London: Tavistock, 1973.

PFEFFER, JEFFREY. "Management as Symbolic Action." *Research in Organizational Behavior,* vol. 3, ed. Larry L. Cummings and Barry M. Shaw. Greenwich, Conn.: JAI Press, 1981.

PFEFFER, JEFFREY and JERRY SALANCIK. "Who Gets Power and How They Hold onto It." *Organizational Dynamics 5* (Winter 1977), pp. 3–21.

QUINN, JAMES B. *Strategies for Change: Logical Incrementalism.* Homewood, Ill.: Irwin, 1980.

RISEMAN, DAVID. "Huck Finn, Superman, and the Business Establishment," *Wharton Magazine* (Winter 1979).

ROETHLISBERGER, FRITZ and WILLIAM DICKSON. *Management and the Worker.* Cambridge, Mass.: Harvard University Press, 1939.

ROSENBAUM, JAMES E. "Tournament Mobility: Career Patterns in a Corporation," *Administrative Science Quarterly* (June 1979).

ROWAN, ROY. "Hunches Are More Than Blind Faith," *Fortune* (April 23, 1979).

RUMULT, RICHARD. *Strategy, Structure, and Economic Performance.* Boston: Harvard Business School, 1974.

SAYLES, LEONARD. *Managerial Behavior.* New York: McGraw-Hill, 1964.

SCHEIN, ED. *Organizational Psychology.* Englewood Cliffs, N.J.: Prentice-Hall, 1965.

SCHEIN, ED. "The General Manager: A Profile." Distinguished Management Scholar Lecture given at the Eastern Academy of Management, May 5, 1972.

SCHREISHEIM, CHARLES, JAMES TOLLIVER, and ORLANDO BEHLING. "Leadership Theory: Some Implications for Managers," *MSU Business Topics* (Summer 1978).

SCOTT, BRUCE. "Stages of Corporate Development." Boston: Intercollegiate Case Clearing House, 1971.

SHARTLE, C. L. *Executive Performance and Leadership.* Englewood Cliffs, N.J.: Prentice-Hall, 1956.

SHETTY, Y. K. and N. S. PERRY, JR. "Are Top Executives Transferable Across Companies?" *Business Horizons* (June 1976).

SKINNER, WICK and EARL SASSER. "Managers with Impact: Versatile and Inconsistent," *Harvard Business Review* (November/December 1977).

STEWART, ROSEMARY. "Managerial Agendas—Reactive or Proactive," *Organizational Dynamics* (Autumn 1979).

STEWART, ROSEMARY. "To Understand the Manager's Job: Consider Demands, Constraints, Choices," *Organizational Dynamics* (Spring 1976).

STEWART, ROSEMARY. *Managers and Their Jobs.* New York: Macmillan, 1967.

STEWART, ROSEMARY. *Contrasts in Management.* New York: McGraw-Hill, 1976.

STEWART, ROSEMARY, PETER SMITH, JENNY BLAKE, and PAULINE WINGATE. *The District Administration for the National Health Service.* London: King's Fund, 1980.

STEINBRUNER, JOHN. *The Cybernetic Theory of Decision.* Princeton, N.J.: Princeton University Press, 1974.

STIEGLITZ, HAROLD. "The Chief Executive's Job and the Size of the Company," *The Conference Board Record* (September 1970).

STOGDILL, RALPH M. *Handbook of Leadership.* New York: Free Press, 1974.

STOGDILL, RALPH M. and A. E. COONS. *Leader Behavior: Its Description and Measurement.* Columbus, O.: Ohio State University, Bureau of Business Research, 1957.

STRONG, E. K., JR. *Vocational Interests 18 Years After College.* Minneapolis: University of Minnesota Press, 1955.

SUSSMAN, JOHN A. "Making it to the Top: A Career Profile of the Senior Executive," *Management Review* (July 1979).

THOMPSON, JAMES. *Organizations in Action.* Englewood Cliffs, N.J.: Prentice-Hall, 1967.

TOLLIVER, J. and O. BEHLING. "Leadership Theory: Some Implications for Managers," *MSU Business Topics* (Summer 1978).

TREWARTHA, ROBERT L. and M. GENE NEWPORT. *Management.* Dallas: Business Publications, Inc., 1976.

UYTERHOEVEN, HUGO. "General Managers in the Middle." *Harvard Business Review* (March/April 1972).

VROOM, VICTOR and PHILLIP YETTON. *Leadership and Decision-Making.* Pittsburgh: University of Pittsburgh Press, 1973.

Wall Street Journal. "More Companies Looking Within for Managers," October 28, 1980, p. 37.

Wall Street Journal. "Some Companies Try to Spot Leaders Early and Guide Them to the Top" (February 25, 1981).

WHITE, ROBERT W. *Lives in Progress.* New York: Holt, Rinehart and Winston, 1966.

WHYTE, WILLIAM. *Street Corner Society.* Chicago: University of Chicago Press, 1943.

WORTMAN, MAX. *Defining the Manager's Job.* New York: AMACOM, 1975.

Wrapp, H. Edward. "Good Managers Don't Make Policy Decisions," *Harvard Business Review* (September/October 1967).

ZALEZNIK, ABRAHAM. *Human Dilemmas of Leadership.* New York: Harper and Row, 1967.

INDEX

Index _____